*B*REAKING *T*HROUGH

Creating Opportunities for America's Woman and Minority-Owned Businesses

SECOND EDITION

Susan Phillips Bari

Women's Business Enterprise
National Council

WBEN C

Creating Opportunities…Recognizing Excellence

Published by the Women's Business Enterprise National Council
(WBENC)
1120 Connecticut Avenue, NW
Suite 1000
Washington DC, 20036

First Edition: June 2004
Second Edition: March 2006

Please visit www.WBENC.org for more information about WBENC
or to order additional copies of this book. WBENC offers special
quantity discounts for bulk purchase. Excerpts of this book may be
used with written consent from WBENC.

Library of Congress Control Number: 2005938280

ISBN: 0-9753928-2-4

Printed in the United States of America
Published in Washington, DC

Praise for the First Edition

"I learned some of the best tips for getting in contact with the companies I want to do business with by reading *Breaking Through*."
—Janet Carabelli, President, IdealogyCreative

"I have read *Breaking Through* cover to cover—what a jewel. I cannot wait for the next edition. I have recommended this book to every women business owner I know."
—Julia M. Rhodes, President/CEO,
KleenSlate Concepts, LLC

"*Breaking Through* was very helpful to these African American Women Business Owners as they start the journey to increasing corporate business."
—Tanya Penny, Vice President, Procurement, MCI

"*Breaking Through* is so practical, grounded and REAL! I love the generosity with which Susan Bari shared her own experience. It just makes the advice ring so true."
—Margaret Heffernan, Author, *The Naked Truth:*
A Working Woman's Manifesto on Business
and What Really Matters and CEO, iCast

"The table of contents in *Breaking Through* is chock full of very interesting topics that will definitely help me to strengthen and expand my business."
—Michael A. Tyus, President and CEO,
Aurora Consulting Group, LLC

"*Breaking Through* is very well organized and informative, and its writing style makes it fun to read!"
—Alisa Hall, President, Down To Earth Naturals

"*Breaking Through* is superb and exactly what the aspiring entrepreneurs need. The examples bring home the reality of tremendous opportunities that exist! I ordered 50 copies!"
—Himanshu Bhatia, CEO, Rose International

To my husband Dick, whose loyalty, patience, love and advice help me to be the best that I can be.

Table of Contents

Acknowledgments

People always ask me, "When do you find the time to write books?" I know that every author says so, but it is true that this book is truly a collaborative effort and owes its completion to each and every one of the women business owners, WBENC Board of Directors members, corporate members, women's business organization executives and WBENC staff who have contributed their advice and anecdotes to these pages.

While each person's contribution is unique and appreciated, special thanks go to:

My collaborator, Lindsey Pollak. I ran into Lindsey at an Office Depot Success Strategies for Businesswomen conference (see the chapter on networking) and she told me that she had just published a book. "I have always wanted to write a book," I said. "Then why don't you? I can help," she replied. Lindsey likes to call herself a "book coach" and she is certainly that and more. Over the phone, on the internet and with coffee dates at Starbucks, Lindsey helped me to organize the content of the book, devised a schedule for writing, editing and publishing and kept me to it.

My good friend and colleague, Ginger Conrad. When frequent author WBE Elizabeth Kearney advised me to try to have a sample chapter published in a magazine as a "teaser" for the book, I turned to Ginger, the publisher of *MBE Magazine*. Not only did she agree to my request, but she also volunteered to read and edit the book before it went to press and served on the focus group that reviewed title options. She has also edited this second, revised edition.

WBENC's director of marketing and communications, Danielle Walton, has served as WBENC's publisher, following in the footsteps of Leslie Magliocchetti who worked on the first edition. Danielle handles all of the nuts and bolts issues of copyrights, designers and printers. Danielle has brought our publishing processes up to date and found a new, WBE printer, Docunetworks, led by President Wendy N. Morical.

I also want to thank my family. Both my maternal and paternal grandfathers came to this country as immigrants at the dawn of the last century and found the American dream through business ownership. Their entrepreneurial genes were passed down to me—the greatest inheritance a person can claim.

When I was in the fourth grade, my mother, a night owl who stayed up to watch late night television, stopped getting up to make my breakfast and turned that task over to my Dad. My father was a small business owner who, along with omelets and eggs over easy, for the next eight years shared with me the ups and downs of entrepreneurship. He taught me about clients who did not pay their bills, changes in the economy, lines of credit from banks and employee problems. He also shared the pride of building a business, providing employment and opportunity for his staff and creating a secure future for our family. When I left a teaching career in a top-notch school system to become a manufacturers' representative, my mother was horrified and my Dad was proud. He advised me to always act ethically in business dealings, never split a commission or lie about a product's capabilities and to always emphasize customer service.

My husband Dick has been both an "intrapreneur" (an innovator within an organization) and entrepreneur and his most important role is chair of my fan club. Without his support and patience, the "free" time to write and revise this book would not have been possible.

Today, as a social entrepreneur, I am grateful that I love what I do, that I enjoy and am fulfilled by my work and that I like and respect all of my colleagues associated with WBENC.

Finally, I want to thank Cendant Car Rental Group for sponsoring the second edition of *Breaking Through*. They have been committed supporters of WBENC, and, more importantly, of women business enterprises, for a very long time and we are honored to have them as our sponsor.

Foreword

"Diversity today for a competitive advantage tomorrow."

The motto of Avis's supplier diversity program says it all. A diversified supply chain is crucial to our company's growth and to the growth of any company in the increasingly global economy of the twenty-first century. Forward-thinking businesses that do not diversify their supply chains and make opportunities available to woman- and minority-owned businesses will miss out on the innovations, new products and ideas offered by these suppliers, and will therefore be at a competitive disadvantage in the marketplace.

Here at Avis we recognize that, in addition to offering advantages as suppliers, small business owners and their employees are an enormous component of our customer base. Further, women business owners continue to be the fastest-growing segment of the entrepreneurial economy. We initiated our supplier diversity program in 1996 with a team of one: Lynn Boccio. Today, we have an entire department dedicated to supplier diversity.

That is why this Second Edition of *Breaking Through: Creating Opportunities for America's Woman and Minority-Owned Businesses* comes at an important time. New markets are opening up every day—new consumer segments, new business categories, emerging countries—and more and more companies are recognizing the need to find new and different suppliers that meet the specialized needs of these new markets. As you will read in the following pages, there are many opportunities for women and minority businesses to win contracts from major corporations, and from each other.

While these opportunities exist, competition among suppliers is fierce, and business owners need to find every advantage they can. Enter the Women's Business Enterprise National Council (WBENC), and Susan Phillips Bari, who has created this valuable resource for you. Avis is both a member and participant on the Board of Directors of WBENC, and we are proud to have been listed on WBENC's annual exclusive listing of America's Top Corporations for Women's Business Enterprises. From its inception in 1997, WBENC has taken the lead in creating opportunities for women business owners to grow their businesses through corporate contracts and access to customized information and resources. The thousands of businesses already certified by WBENC understand that certification provides an invaluable competitive advantage.

But certification is only the beginning—women and minority entrepreneurs must combine their certification with smart, innovative strategies. This is what Susan Phillips Bari offers in *Breaking Through*. Inside you will find expert advice on marketing, networking, skills to develop, mistakes to avoid and many detailed stories told by executives and business owners who have successfully navigated the supplier diversity waters.

Like many corporations in America, Avis has undergone many changes over the years. One thing has remained constant, however: our commitment to supplier diversity. And that will never change.

There is no telling exactly what the future will bring in the fast-changing world of American business. But I am confident that WBENC, and women- and minority-owned businesses like yours will be out in front, leading the way.

—F. Robert Salerno
   President and Chief Operating Officer
   Avis Rent A Car System, Inc.

Foreword from the Author

A month before my college graduation in 1967, all seniors were informed we must participate in an "exit interview" with the guidance department. Every woman student heard the same question: "Do you want to be a teacher or a nurse?" If the answer was "neither," the next question was "How many words a minute do you type?" With limited typing skills and no desire to change bedpans, I opted for teaching. My mother and aunts assured me that this was an honorable and rewarding profession that would provide me the flexibility—once I had identified the perfect husband—to be home when my kids returned from school or were on vacation.

I loved teaching and found that it was rewarding as promised. However, after a few years of watching one hundred children go through puberty at 8:00 a.m. every morning, I yearned for more adult interaction. I was also broke and tired of working part-time selling men's shirts to make the living wage I needed to make up for the fact that Mr. Perfect Husband had not yet arrived on the scene.

Eventually, I found a part-time position, after school and on Saturdays, filing and doing other administrative chores for a successful small business owner who served as a manufacturers' representative for several companies. In addition to the linens and domestics lines of merchandise he carried, there was a "piece goods" line of on-the-bolt fabrics. I asked if he could provide me with some sample fabric since I made many of my own clothes. He did me one better and offered to pay me to make "model garments" that he could use as part of his sales pitch ("I have a home-sewer named Susan who samples each of these fabric lines before I show them to you," he would say to clients, "and Susan assures me that this fabric is easy to work with and produces a satisfactory result for the home sewer"). He let me keep the garments once the selling season ended. This arrangement worked well for me. At the time I did not even realize I had just launched my first business!

My business initiation went a step further when I was called upon to make the pitch myself to a buyer who was visiting the office one Saturday morning. After the buyer had signed the largest order to date and left, my boss asked if I would consider leaving my teaching position to join his sales team. At nearly double my then-salary as a teacher, plus the promise of additional commission-based bonuses—and no puberty problems among the buyers I would be calling on—this was an easy decision to make.

I received preliminary training by the manufacturer and then went out on my own to call on buyers for department store chains, "mom and pop" operations and mass merchandisers. I was ecstatic.

Three months later, the IRS came calling on my boss' door. "Last hired, first fired" (yes, me) was the result. I did not know where I would go to find employment, but I did know it would not be back to the schoolhouse. I had caught the business bug.

After several fruitless job interviews (in the early 1970s there were few women in sales in any field), I decided to see if I could start my own manufacturers' representative business. After three days of visiting each of the exhibiting companies at a trade show, I identified six companies that would let me represent them on a commission basis in New England. One even offered a small advance on commission each month to tide me over until the seasonal sales started translating into post-delivery paychecks.

Now I was really in business. I did not know the word at

the time, but I was an *entrepreneur*. I was also the first woman commissioned sales representative in this industry. Amazing— an industry selling fabric to home sewers, 99.9 percent of whom were women—had no women selling its products to the stores. It would be many years before I translated this industry-based perspective into an awareness of the inequities existing for all women in all industries, and felt even more strongly by women of color.

Selling to Big Business

My repping experience taught me another lesson that has expanded over the years and played an important role in my founding of the Women's Business Enterprise National Council (WBENC, pronounced "wee-benk"): It is easier to make a living selling to a mass merchandiser who has 300 stores than to the mom and pop shop on the corner. Bigger contracts are better than smaller contracts. Commissions based on sales to 300 stores resulting from a meeting with one buyer are more efficient and lucrative than commissions based on sales to 300 stores resulting from meetings with 300 buyers.

But, as I quickly learned, it is not easy to get in the door of large corporations to get the bigger contracts. Twenty years later when WBENC was first founded, things had not gotten any easier. For woman- and minority-owned firms who are not part of the old boy's network, this is particularly challenging. I became determined to find my way in.

I first heard about the existence of supplier diversity programs in 1994. They are departments that exist in many large American corporations to create mutually beneficial business relationships between previously "disadvantaged" women and minority business owners and large corporations that can purchase their products and services. Supplier diversity departments serve as internal advocates for diverse business owners. I quickly determined that these programs represented an enormous opportunity to level the playing field for woman entrepreneurs like me. Their existence provides an extraordinary new "door" to opportunity. However, I soon discovered that too few woman- and minority-owned firms knew of, or took advantage of, this marketing opportunity.

At the time, the National Minority Supplier Development Council (NMSDC) had already been founded (in 1972) to vet and certify minority business enterprises, and to help minority business owners access the opportunities in the corporate market, but no organization existed to help women grow their businesses through corporate opportunities.

In 1997, with the support of eleven forward thinking corporations, four women's business organizations, and many dedicated women business owners, we launched the Women's Business Enterprise National Council (WBENC). Our goal was, and still is, to enhance opportunities for women's business enterprises in America's major business markets—to help women find the doors to opportunity and break through those doors to achieve enormous growth and success.

WBENC certifies thousands of woman-owned businesses each year (verifying that they are at least 51 percent woman-owned and operated) through programs in fourteen regionally based organizations, and then helps connect those certified woman-owned businesses with corporate purchasing officers. Our website, Internet database, conferences and business fairs provide opportunities for major corporations and woman-owned businesses to meet and do business with each other. Our educational programs, such as the Tuck-WBENC Executive Program presented with the Tuck School of Business at Dartmouth and underwritten by IBM, provide the tools for women business owners to grow their management skills along with their new contract opportunities. The tips, stories, advice and insights I have collected as WBENC President are presented in this book.

I am grateful that I have been able to translate my entrepreneurial impulses to "social entrepreneurship" as the leader of a nonprofit organization dedicated to providing assistance in the form of opportunity to other women entrepreneurs. WBENC has grown through the participation of America's largest and most respected companies, who share our commitment to women's business growth. Through WBENC and our friendship with the NMSDC, I am now able to help woman- and minority-owned businesses develop growth strategies based on the marketing insight that I developed selling piece goods many years ago. With this book, I can now bring these strategies, tools and opportunities to an even larger audience: women and minority business owners like you.

Breaking Through: Creating Opportunities for America's Woman and Minority-Owned Businesses provides you with an overview of the huge opportunities available through supplier diversity programs, and shares my secrets for marketing your business to Fortune 1000 companies and keeping the business you acquire. Selling to corporate America is not easy, but it is the key to extraordinary growth for your business and our national economy.

—*Susan Phillips Bari*

Introduction

Did you know that more than 23 million businesses compose the United States business landscape? Yet, of these 23 million, there are, of course, only 1,000 companies in the famous Fortune 1000 list of major corporations. We frequently forget that each and every one of those big companies started as a small business, and more importantly, that these large companies need to do business with smaller companies in order to survive and thrive.

The Fortune 1000 started with visionary entrepreneurs who risked their resources and reputations to build corporations that provide each of us with everything from cell phone service to the computers on our desktops to the wheels on our luggage to air conditioning in our offices and cars, and the cars themselves. Like most of us who have started companies, these entrepreneurs used personal savings, a mortgage on their homes, or even their personal credit cards to provide the start-up funds necessary to begin operations. Breaking through the barriers in their paths from dreams to great riches and professional recognition required access to capital, the ear of investors and an open door to purchasing officials who could buy or invest in *their* products. And, perhaps most important, they required a strong strategy for success.

It is to the last business need that this book is dedicated: finding the right strategies to open doors, find supporters, and gain access to growth opportunities for women and minority business owners. While access to capital is crucial for small business growth and success, *Breaking Through* focuses on helping small and medium-sized businesses secure contracts with large corporations—the big sales that lead to enormous and lasting growth. But big opportunity does not guarantee big success. You need smart strategies.

How do you, as a small or medium-sized business owner, build a strategy to do business with the Fortune 1000? Here comes the good news: If you are one of over 11 million women or minority business owners in the United States, you have a unique opportunity: corporate supplier diversity programs, which will be explained in depth shortly. *Breaking Through* offers insider information on these programs and how they can help you grow your business. Beyond information, the following pages provide proven marketing strategies specifically crafted to maximize supplier diversity opportunities for your company. *Breaking Through* is the competitive advantage you need to do business with corporate America.

Where Are We Now? The Status of Woman- and Minority-owned Business in America

Woman-owned and woman-led firms represent a most promising segment of our national economy. According to the Center for Women's Business Research, they outpaced other U.S. businesses in both growth and economic contribution from 1997 to 2004. During this time period, woman-owned firms (with 51 percent or more ownership by a woman or women) grew at nearly two and a half times the rate of all U.S. privately held firms (23 percent vs. 9 percent). They are generating nearly $1.2 trillion in revenues. And, they provide jobs for 9.8 million people.

What else defines these businesses? They are small, medium and large; rural, suburban and urban; product and service-based; family owned and global; product and service-oriented; non-traditional and everything in between. The diversity of woman-owned businesses selling to corporate America is truly astounding. This book will share strategies of WBENC-certified businesses ranging from sole proprietorships to multinational corporations as large as Carlson Companies, a multi-billion dollar enterprise whose subsidiaries include Carlson Marketing Group, Radisson Hotels & Resorts, Radisson Seven Seas Cruises, T.G.I. Friday's and Carlson Wagonlit Travel, all ably led by Marilyn Carlson Nelson.

Minority businesses, too, are rapidly accessing the American dream through entrepreneurship. According to the U.S. Census Bureau, from 1997 to 2002, the number of businesses owned by Asians grew by 24 percent, while African-American minority businesses grew by 45 percent. Hispanic minority businesses grew by 31 percent. Together, women and minorities compose nearly 50 percent of all small businesses in the United States. Millions of Americans report for work each day in a company owned by a woman or minority CEO. They pay for their mortgages, children's tuition and summer vacations with salaries paid by a woman- or minority-owned firm.

How have women and minority businesses grown so large? Marilyn Carlson Nelson and Carlson Companies found their spectacular success by helping others succeed—by franchising successful business models, directly serving the needs of a "who's who" of global corporations, even helping those corporations build better relationships with their own customers. David Steward, whose World Wide Technology is one of America's largest African American owned businesses, has carved out a major niche in the telecommunications industry.

The world is waiting for more Marilyn Carlson Nelsons and David Stewards. As of 2005, nine *Fortune* 500 companies are run by women, and a total of 19 *Fortune* 1000 companies have women CEOs. Not interested in leading the next IBM? Growth opportunities abound at all levels. This book will help you expand your company in size, scope and influence whether you are looking for a $1,000 contract or a $100 million dollar contract. The world of business is changing, and woman- and minority-owned businesses like yours are on the cutting edge at every level.

Changing the Language: "Growth Market Enterprises"

As we begin to dig deeper into the supplier diversity landscape, it is important to pause for a moment to define our terms. Thus far I have referred to "woman- and minority-owned businesses," a somewhat unwieldy phrase that begs the question, What if a business owner is both a woman *and* a minority? The nation's Latina business owners—a group starting businesses at a whopping six times the rate of all other companies—would certainly question this limiting terminology. WBENC-certified business owner Annette Taddeo, CEO of LanguageSpeak, Inc., resents even the term "minority" and states, "There is nothing minor about me."

Consider this comprehensive list of the current supplier diversity categories. Notice the breadth, and complexity, of the current terminology:

Cheat Sheet: Supplier Diversity Classifications

Minority Business Enterprise (MBE): A for-profit enterprise currently located in the United States or its trust territories, and is at least 51 percent owned by African Americans, Hispanic Americans, Native Americans, Asian-Indian Americans or Asian-Pacific Americans. Individual(s) must be involved in the day-to-day management of the business.

African Americans are U.S. citizens whose origins are in any Black racial groups of Africa.

Hispanic Americans are U.S. citizens whose origins are in South America, Central America, Mexico, Cuba, the Dominican Republic, Puerto Rico, or the Iberian Peninsula, including Portugal.

Native Americans are American Indians, Inuit, Aleuts, and Native Hawaiians.

Asian-Indian Americans are U.S. citizens whose origins are in India, Pakistan, Bangladesh, Sri Lanka, Bhutan, or Nepal.

Asian-Pacific Americans are U.S. citizens whose origins are in Japan, China, the Philippines, Vietnam, Korea, Samoa, Guam, the U.S. Trust Territory of the Pacific Islands (Republic of Palau), the Northern Mariana Islands, Laos, Kampuchea (Cambodia), Taiwan, Burma, Thailand, Malaysia, Indonesia, Singapore, Brunei, Republic of the Marshall Islands, or the Federated States of Micronesia.

Woman Business Enterprise (WBE): A for-profit enterprise currently located in the United States or its trust territories, and is at least 51 percent owned, controlled, and operated by a woman or women of U.S. citizenship. Individual(s) must be involved in the day-to-day management of the business. Disadvantaged Business Enterprise (DBE): A small business owned and controlled by socially and economically disadvantaged individuals, primarily minorities and women

Disabled Business Enterprise: A for-profit enterprise currently located in the United States or its trust territories, and is at least 51 percent owned by an individual(s) of U.S. citizenship with a permanent physical or mental impairment which substantially

limits one or more of such persons' major life activities.
Individual(s) must be involved in the day-to-day management of
the business.

Disabled Veteran Business Enterprise (DVBE): A for-profit enterprise currently located in the United States or its trust territories,
and is at least 51 percent owned by an individual(s) who has
performed active service in one of the United States armed services and is disabled as defined above. Individual(s) must be
involved in the day-to-day management of the business.

Veteran Owned Small Business (VOSB): A small business (as
defined pursuant to Section 3 of the Small Business Act) currently
located in the United States or its trust territories, and is at least
51 percent owned by an individual(s) who has performed active
service in one of the United States armed services.
HUBZone (HUB): A small business located in a HUBZone
(Historically Underutilized Business Zone), owned and controlled
by one or more U.S. citizens, with at least 35 percent of its
employees residing in a HUBZone. (To learn if you are located in
a HUBZone, visit http://map.sba.gov/hubzone/init.asp#address.)
- Adapted from the Citigroup Supplier Diversity Website www.citi-
group.com/citigroup/corporate/supplier_diversity/def.htm

Complicated, right? With this book I propose renaming *all*
of the above-mentioned businesses as **Growth Market
Enterprises (GMEs)**. This term captures the present and future
of the new face of business in America. Growth Market Enterprise
also communicates the powerful role these diverse businesses
play in the economic health of our nation today and into the
future. The new name also provides a realistic and positive
descriptive that connotes business capability, progress and deliv-
erability. These businesses are not "disadvantaged" or "minor,"
but represent the new demographic landscape of both America's

business community and the country's consumer base. They reflect the diversity and promise of our country.

Furthermore, GME incorporates women, minority and other identifications, combining several very powerful communities and building strength in our combined numbers. While you will not see the term GME used in corporate or government supplier diversity literature, I will use the phrase throughout this book as the most inclusive way to define the businesses that can benefit from corporate supplier diversity initiatives and the strategies I will recommend.

The Case for "Growth Market Enterprise"

A 2004 survey of WBENC corporate members and certified WBEs found strong support for a change in terminology:

- 89 percent of WBEs would prefer to identify themselves as a Growth Market Enterprise (rather than a WBE) when introducing themselves to potential clients or bidding for contracts.

- 96 percent of WBEs believe the term Growth Market Enterprise makes the best impression on new or potential clients/customers (compared to the term WBE).

- When asked about a range of positive characteristics that might describe Growth Market Enterprises and Disadvantaged Business Enterprises, only a quarter (25 percent) of WBEs would characterize a Disadvantaged Business Enterprise as "expert in its field," compared to more than two thirds (68 percent) who would characterize a Growth Market Enterprise as "expert in its field."

The Big Opportunity: Supplier Diversity Programs

"Great, I identify as a GME and I would love to sell my widgets at Office Depot," you say, "but how do I get a foot, or even a toe, in the door—and where exactly is the door?" The answer is that the "door" to opportunity for GMEs is the corporate supplier diversity marketplace.

Supplier diversity programs are corporate initiatives that create mutually beneficial business relationships between GMEs and large corporations that can purchase their products and services. In other words, corporations promise to buy a certain percentage of their products and services from woman- and minority-owned firms. These programs were designed in the 1970s and 1980s to help level the playing field for businesses previously ignored by traditionally white, male-dominated corporations. Smart companies understand that their customer bases are made up of women and minority consumers, so their vendor bases should be, too.

When your business is certified as "woman-owned" and/or "minority-owned" (as I have mentioned, there is no official "GME" certification today, although I will use this new term throughout the book), you gain a marketing advantage by qualifying to participate in supplier diversity programs. With WBE (Woman Business Enterprise) or MBE (Minority Business Enterprise) certification, you have an extra door open to you in the corporate purchasing process. Of course, this does not guarantee a contract or any special treatment. Your product must be of the highest standards, your price competitive and your service exemplary. Certification as a WBE or MBE is only the beginning.

Breaking Through shares the secrets—the pitches, the proposals, the tips, the marketing plans, the technology platforms—of entrepreneurs who have built successful businesses by including supplier diversity programs in their growth strategy.

Their tactics, strategies, successes—and their mistakes—will provide you with a blueprint for making supplier diversity work for you. Remember, with over 11 million woman- and minority-owned businesses in the United States, there is a lot of competition, and you must differentiate your business, even when you are using the connections and opportunities afforded by supplier diversity contacts. How do you break through?

In Chapter One, you will learn everything there is to know about supplier diversity programs: what they are, who runs them, how long they have been around and how you, the entrepreneur, can find them in your industry. The best supplier diversity programs include outreach to GMEs, information on how to do business with the corporation, assistance in identifying the correct departmental buyer and the appropriate timing for a marketing call; but every program is different. Interviews with representatives from some of America's leading companies will provide you with an insider's view of how these departments really work across a broad array of industries, and how they want to work with you.

Next, in Chapter Two, you will learn the essential first building block to supplying corporate America: certification. Supplier diversity programs usually require that you be "certified" as a woman or minority-owned business enterprise, validating that your company is 51 percent owned, managed and controlled by a woman or minority. They rely on independent, third party organizations such as the Women's Business Enterprise National Council (WBENC) for women and the National Minority Supplier Development Council (NMSDC) for minorities to conduct the certification process. This chapter provides a concise and easy-to-understand explanation of how you can obtain and maintain your certification as a WBE, MBE or both. The process will be reviewed and a check list provided for the documents you should organize before starting the certification process.

Chapter Three provides information on targeting your marketing strategy to take full advantage of your GME status. This chapter will share the marketing plans and outreach strategies of successful certified businesses.

In real estate, they say, "location, location, location." For business owners, the chant is, "network, network, network." Chapter Four of *Breaking Through* shows you how and tells you where. Attendance at business fairs and buyers' marts (sponsored by women's or minority business organizations and corporations) provide access to purchasing professionals who want to buy from you—not sell to you, as is true at many other trade fairs and conferences. Relationships are crucial to GME success and networking is the way to build strong contacts.

Chapters Five offers advanced strategies for certified businesses, such as strategic alliances and Second Tier supplying. This chapter explains the many doors available for suppliers wanting to do business with corporate America so readers can explore every possible opportunity.

Chapters Six, Seven and Eight explore the three "Ps" of supplier diversity – preparation, pitching and perseverance. In Chapter Six, you will prepare to ask and answer the right questions to win business from a large corporation. This includes establishing your pricing and knowing your technological capabilities.

Chapter Seven discusses the second "P," pitching. This chapter outlines the importance of developing and practicing key messages to seal the deal. Remember, you may have only a few minutes to explain what your business does and why the person you are speaking with should be interested. Experts provide tips on how to create presentations that distinguish your product or service from the competition, and comfortably incorporate your GME status into your sales pitch.

Chapter Eight shares several stories of the perseverance and patience required to do business with corporate America. For go-go-go entrepreneurs, this can be the most challenging aspect of the process.

Finally, Chapter Nine of *Breaking Through* will help you keep the contracts you secure. Making the client's goals your goals is key to building long-term relationships and long-term success.

Breaking Through: Creating Opportunities for America's Woman and Minority-Owned Businesses is your partner in business growth. It can be read and re-read at every stage of the development of your company, from start-up to becoming a Fortune 1000 business yourself. Refer to the stories, tips, and checklists on the following pages whenever you find yourself at a crossroads or in need of support and inspiration. The goal of this book is to help Growth Market Enterprises like yours achieve the amazing expansion of which you are capable. *Breaking Through* will help make you and your company the big business success story of the next decade.

Chapter One

Big Bucks from Big Business

If you are a woman or minority business owner, there is no greater opportunity to grow your business than to access the corporate market. This holds true no matter what product or service you offer, and no matter how big or small your company. The best news of all is that, if you take advantage of the recommendations in this book and become involved in corporate supplier diversity programs and certification organizations, you will find enormous support along the way.

Whether you are entirely new to supplier diversity initiatives or you are a certified pro, this chapter provides an essential overview of the ever-growing supplier diversity industry. I will share an insider's guide to the "who, what, when, where, why and how" of corporate supplier diversity programs. You should master the information in this chapter before you approach any company as a potential vendor.

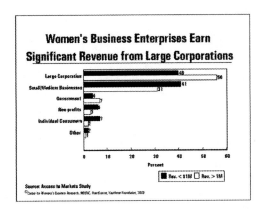

As you can see in the preceding chart, corporations represent a significant portion of revenue for women business owners. According to WBENC's 2003 *Access to Markets Survey*:

- 56 percent of the revenues of women's business enterprises with $1 million or more in sales came from large corporations.
- 40 percent of the revenues of companies with revenues below $1 million came from large corporations.

Do not wait another minute to join this community. For a full list of corporations that currently accept WBENC Certification, visit *www.wbenc.org/opportunities/certification.html*.

FAQ: Could my company really win a contract with a large corporation?

Women and minority business owners new to the world of supplier diversity are often surprised at the range of businesses—from sole proprietorships to multi-million dollar companies—supplying to large corporations through this exciting door to opportunity. Here are just a few examples; many more success stories appear throughout the book:

- Barbara Singer, a New York-based photographer, won a contract to take headshots of executives at Pfizer.
- Linda Laino started her company, Festive Productions, as a small DJ business in Long Island, New York. Upon encouragement from Lynn Boccio, vice president, Strategic Business and Diversity Relations of Avis Rent A Car and Budget Rent A Car, Festive became certified and is now a successful production company creating large-scale events for such companies as Avis and Hertz.
- Anastasia Kostoff-Mann, chairman and founder of The

Corniche Group, based in West Hollywood, California, provides travel management to the Los Angeles Dodgers, thanks to the recommendation of Major League Baseball to become certified.

- Bonnie O'Malley and Cindy Sedlmeyer's Branford, Connecticut-based business, ExhibitEase LLC, designs exhibit booths, banners, graphics and visual presentations for corporations such as Colgate, Major League Baseball and Pfizer, as well as designing a display for their local certification organization, the Women Presidents' Educational Organization.

- Nina Eisenman, president of Eisenman Associates, a graphic design firm in New York City, won contracts to design and produce the annual reports of UST and PepsiCo, and to design and produce a brochure for Aetna.

- Betty Lau, co-founder of Applied Information Services in Somerset, New Jersey, provides customized software development, e-commerce and Internet technology solutions for such clients as Prudential Financial, Johnson Controls and Motorola.

- Diana Conley left an elementary school teaching career to start her Illinois-based company, ComputerLand - Downers Grove. Her staff is vendor-trained and service authorized for sales, installation and repair of PC equipment. IBM uses her company as a subcontractor for many projects.

- Lynn Griffith, president of Welcome Florida, provides corporate destination management for companies including Office Depot, Coca Cola and Travelers.

- Sherra Aguirre's company, Aztec Facility Services, based in Houston, Texas, provides housekeeping, landscaping, window cleaning, carpet cleaning and related facility maintenance services for Fortune 500 clients.

- Rita Meyers is president and her daughter, Stacy Ames, is vice president of Falmer Thermal Spray, a 43-year-old WBE-certified full-service thermal spray coating operation based in Lynn, Massachusetts. Customers include Raytheon, Invensys, MIT Lincoln Laboratories and Osram Sylvania.

- Betsy Mordecai, president of Denver, Colorado-based MorSports & Events, was encouraged by MasterCard to apply for certification, then received a three-year contract to provide special events and meeting planning services for the company.

- Amy Birnbaum, CEO of Royal Coachman Worldwide, provides limousine service, employee shuttles and chauffeured ground transportation services for such companies as Cendant Corporation, Pfizer, Avon, Citigroup, Honeywell and Novartis.

And...Who Woulda Thought?

Here are some surprising products that led their producers to huge procurement contracts:

- The U.S. Defense Department, for example, purchases dog collars from a GME in Martinsburg, West Virginia.

- Harley Davidson buys leather "thong" cell phone holders from Niki Beavers of Jeva Technologies, a GME in Hillsboro, Florida.

WHY is there a need for supplier diversity programs?

"As large company buyers, we set up barriers that we do not even know we are raising. We have to make a special effort to go beyond doing business as usual. Supplier diversity programs are the way we make certain the barriers come down."
- *Jerry Martin, former senior vice president, Global Purchasing, Frito-Lay*

As defined in the Introduction, supplier diversity programs are corporate initiatives to create mutually beneficial business relationships between previously disadvantaged Growth Market Enterprises (such as women, ethnic minorities and disabled business owners) and large corporations that can purchase their products and services. While many companies have a lot of catching up to do, at least 350 of the Fortune 500 are eager to do business with diverse suppliers like you.

Supplier diversity programs also exist because smart corporations know that the demographics of the American economic landscape have changed dramatically and they must do business with the diverse groups that represent their supplier and customer base today and into the future. Besides the fact that women and minorities are starting businesses at a rapid pace, we are also growing by leaps and bounds in number and in consumer power. Corporate America cannot afford to lose our business. Consider these numbers:

- African American consumers represented $631 billion in buying power in 2002, spending $130 billion on housing, $52.4 billion on food, $48.7 billion on cars and trucks and $14.5 billion on health care.[i]
- The Hispanic and Asian-American populations in the United States are expected to *triple* by 2050.[ii]
- The buying power of Hispanics was $653 billion in 2003 and is expected to grow more than that of any other group in the next 10 years.[iii]
- American women overall spend more than $3.7 trillion a year, making them the largest consumer nation in the world!

Why am I so passionate about the opportunity for GMEs to do business with corporate America? Because we can! The numbers prove that we are only at the tip of the iceberg: The Center for Women's Business Research has documented that more than one-third of all businesses in the United States are woman-owned. They are capable of providing a much larger share of the contractual needs of corporate America—currently accounting for less than four percent of corporate procurement. According to the NMSDC, minorities represent 28 percent of the population of the United States, but minority businesses represent only 15 percent of total businesses and three percent of gross receipts.

At the top of the list of those companies that "get it" is Avis Rent A Car and Budget Rent A Car, formerly part of the Cendant Car Rental Group (CCRG). The program, started by Lynn Boccio in 1996, has grown to five dedicated staff members and its diversity spend has significantly increased in the past decade. How does the company demonstrate its commitment? Avis was the first corporation to start with DivTRAK, a state-of-the-art tracking system that monitors supplier diversity performance. The company sponsors and/or supplier diversity staff attend over thirty national and regional conferences and trade shows annually in connection with the Supplier Diversity Program. Team members serve on the boards of various advocacy organizations, as well as on planning and project committees. And, according to Lynn Boccio, "Our president, Robert Salerno, and senior management totally support the concept and everyday efforts regarding supplier diversity in all aspects of the business."

As you can see, some companies are "getting it right" when it comes to supplier diversity. More and more companies improve their initiatives every day, and it is worth noting which companies are making an effort to create a strong supplier diversity program when you are deciding which corporations to target as prospects. Look to the WBENC and the NMSDC websites for news on corporations that are implementing new programs, or companies excelling with existing programs. The NMSDC names a Corporation of the Year and WBENC presents America's Top Corporations for Women's Business Enterprises annually.

Affiliates of the NMSDC and WBENC honor companies on a regional level as well.

WHAT defines a corporate supplier diversity program?

Corporate supplier diversity programs vary from company to company, but their function is to serve as internal advocates for women and minority suppliers. Consider the mission statement of the UPS Supplier Diversity Program:

> "We provide access and equal opportunity to diverse suppliers and promote and develop these suppliers within and outside our organization. We are committed to ensuring that our Supplier Diversity Process strengthens the small, minority- and woman-owned businesses that drive economic development in the communities we serve."

As you can see, the goal of UPS and other corporate supplier diversity programs is to *help you succeed.*

Specifically, supplier diversity programs incorporate a combination of the following elements:

- **Outreach** – Corporate supplier diversity professionals actively seek relationships with diverse suppliers like you. They find GMEs through involvement with minority and business development organizations (see Chapter Four for more details on various associations and networking groups), participation in various business fair activities and creation and maintenance of informational websites that solicit diverse vendors. Often they will identify appropriate GMEs as soon as they hear of a Request for Proposal (RFP) somewhere in their organization.
- **Certification** – Corporations verify that businesses seeking

to participate in their supplier diversity programs meet the criteria of ownership, management and control to qualify for their initiatives. Many companies offer certification workshops and training or partner with recognized certifying organizations like WBENC and the NMSDC to help facilitate the certification process. (The next chapter will walk you through the certification process in detail.)

- **Qualification** – Supplier diversity staff review the capabilities of GME businesses and refer them to appropriate purchasers for consideration as vendors.

- **Development** – They also review additional needs of GME suppliers and explore ways to provide assistance to them through training, education and, in some cases, formal mentoring. Supplier diversity professionals help GMEs define their value propositions, often advising GMEs on how to better manage cost, margin and price variables.

- **Utilization** – Supplier diversity staff participate in the purchasing process, partnering with purchasing managers in the department needing your product or service. For instance, if you are a temporary staffing company, your supplier diversity contact would facilitate your relationship with the company's Human Resources department and other specific areas that need temporary workers. IT staffing in particular has become a major area of opportunity for GMEs.

- **Tracking** – Supplier diversity departments monitor and report on supplier diversity practices to achieve the company's targets and continually improve results. Most companies set goals for their diversity initiatives that must be met on an annual basis. Typically, today's corporations utilize sophisticated databases that "scrub" procurement lists to identify which of their current and prospective suppliers are woman- or minority-owned and what certifications those companies hold.

Progressive companies monitor their success in supplier diversity through various benchmarking procedures. In 2004, WBENC issued a "Balanced Score Card" (featured in Appendix A) for use by its corporate members in evaluating their progress toward internal goals. One of WBENC's corporate members, Eva Chess of RR Donnelley, recently commented that the score card tool, a benefit offered by WBENC to its corporate members, was alone worth the cost of her annual dues to our organization. WBENC actively supports tracking so we can guide certified WBEs to committed companies, and "encourage" other companies to improve their practices.

HOW do I decide which corporations to target?

Tip #1: Look for customers committed to supplier diversity.

As you are beginning to see, some corporations are more committed to supplier diversity than others. I highly recommend that you begin your process of targeting potential corporate customers by researching which companies foster strong supplier diversity programs. These are the companies who will be most receptive to the strategies outlined in this book.

How do you begin to research corporations that might be potential customers for your particular products or services? The first point of entry I always recommend is the Internet. Virtually every corporate supplier diversity department in the country offers an informative website that tells you most of what you will need to know to make your initial approach. It is a good idea to visit as many supplier diversity websites as possible to review various program structures. The more information you can gather, the better.

I also recommend using search engines such as Google,

entering key words from your business (e.g. software, marketing, electrical components, administrative services, etc.) and the words "supplier diversity."

As we will explore in Chapter Three, corporate supplier diversity websites feature lists of what, when and how they buy from GMEs. I recommend compiling a notebook or individual files containing information and notes about each company's supplier diversity program so you can keep track of your prospects. Some websites offer downloadable reports and information that may be easier to digest offline. It is also smart to keep a list of any GME suppliers featured as "success stories" (a popular feature of many supplier diversity websites), as you may want to make contact with some of the owners of these businesses as you progress through the process of becoming a supplier.

Tip #2: Get involved early and often.

The Internet is a necessary and helpful first step in your research, but you must accompany your online efforts with offline endeavors. While much of the supplier diversity process now takes place online (see later chapters on certification and technology), face-to-face interaction is still a significant component of the purchasing process.

The best way to research supplier diversity opportunities offline is to become involved with one of the many organizations that provide educational and networking opportunities for GMEs. Chapter Four will recommend many strategies for networking in the supplier diversity community, but your first stop should be your local or regional affiliate of WBENC or the NMSDC. While you may already be a member of your industry association, many GMEs have never connected with the supplier diversity factions of their membership organizations. Ask your association contacts to introduce you to any supplier diversity or procurement professionals in the organization as you begin to explore this new business opportunity.

To find even more face-to-face opportunities, pay close attention to calendar listings on the corporate websites you are researching. As mentioned above, many companies' missions include extensive outreach to potential vendors, so they regularly sponsor information sessions and business fairs to provide opportunities for you to meet their staff, purchasing executives, successful GME suppliers, non-profit partners and other experienced professionals who can help you through the process. It is true: companies offer events to educate you on how to sell to them! *WBENC-Discuss@wbenc.org*, our listserv for certified WBEs, provides additional information about corporate and government briefings, procurement conferences and business expos. If you are certified by WBENC and keep your online profile up-to-date, you will receive this information as a matter of course. Other associations provide similar informational services as well.

Do not forget to log the information you gather at live events in your trusty notebook containing your Internet research. Be sure to take copious notes—all of this information will be useful as you navigate the supplier diversity process.

WHO works in the supplier diversity field?

The supplier diversity field is a professional industry like any other, with experienced practitioners doing their jobs day-in and day-out. I have talked to some of the top men and women in the field in order to understand the supplier diversity process from their point of view: what their workday looks like; what they look for in a supplier; what impresses them; what annoys them; and what you can do to build a strong relationship with them. Their advice and success secrets appear throughout the book.

In order to succeed as a supplier, you will need to develop close, trusting relationships with the supplier diversity staff at the companies you target. Purchasing professionals regularly cite "strong relationships" as one of the leading success factors for GME suppliers. Supplier diversity managers truly are your allies in the corporate purchasing process. With all that is said about high tech these days, "high touch" is still important in building business relationships, and supplier diversity is no exception.

In fact, I truly believe that *the single most important success factor for GMEs is the building and maintaining of relationships with supplier diversity professionals.* Supplier diversity executives' jobs are to find qualified diverse suppliers for their companies' needs and advocate on behalf of YOU in the corporate purchasing process. The better your relationship with these advocates, the better your chance of being "top-of-mind" when new contracts arise. Do not just take my word for it. WBENC's 2003 *Access to Markets Survey* found that 97 percent of women entrepreneur respondents rated relationships with decision makers as a key success factor in doing business with large corporations.

Many corporations also have purchasing councils and supplier diversity advocates throughout the supply chain to further advocate on your behalf. The supplier diversity executive is in regular contact with these additional individuals, knows what they are looking for and can provide you with fast-lane access to the appropriate buyer. Additionally, supplier diversity executives network across companies and share information about their most successful GME suppliers.

A Day in the Life

It is important to understand the roles and responsibilities of supplier diversity executives so you can help them achieve their goals. While responsibilities vary depending on the level and experience of the executive, consider these elements that might be found in the position description of a supplier diversity executive:

- Identify and build relationships with qualified, diverse suppliers in order to recommend them to purchasers across the corporation. (Many supplier diversity professionals travel extensively to conferences, business fairs, seminars, award banquets, association meetings and activities, presentations and face-to-face meetings with GME suppliers.)
- Sit on the boards or committees of various local, national and regional certification organizations, associations, councils and GME businesses.
- Respond to GME inquiries and work with GMEs to educate them on the needs of the corporation and the requirements for becoming a supplier, including the importance of certification (see Chapter Two). Provide mentoring and advice as appropriate. WBE Linda Laino, CEO of Festive Productions, captures this role of supplier diversity professionals in describing her relationship with Lynn Boccio, vice president, Strategic Business and Diversity Relations, Avis Rent A Car and Budget Rent A Car. "Lynn has taken me by the hand from the beginning, including nominating me to sit on the WBENC National Forum. She is always there to give me advice. If we need anything we call each other, even for recommendation letters. She tells me what she thinks I should be doing differently, and who I should meet. She has taken me by the hand and introduced me to every supplier diversity person she can. She never does not have time for me." As mentioned previously in this chapter, Lynn encouraged Linda to become certified in the first place.
- Train corporate purchasing personnel across the corporation about the need to include GMEs as suppliers.
- Obtain requirements from prime (First Tier) contractors to facilitate Second Tier opportunities for GMEs (see Chapter

Five for more information about Second Tier supplying).

- Manage the supplier diversity website and other program-marketing collateral.
- Track results of the supplier diversity program to meet the company's goals, as set by the company's CEO and senior management.

Cheat Sheet: Getting to Know
Your Supplier Diversity Contacts

Be sure to find out the following information about any supplier diversity professional at the companies you target, and keep this information updated as you move through the process:

- Name: (Never misspell the name of someone you are trying to impress!)
- Title: (Be sure to get this right as well. Titles vary from company to company and change frequently.)
- Company:
- Contact information:
- Preferred method of communication: (e-mail, phone, cell phone?)
- Assistant's name:
- Areas of responsibility: (What internal departments, geographic regions, and/or ethnic markets does this person oversee? Again, responsibilities vary by company.)
- Name of regional or local contact person (if different from above):

WHEN do companies make their purchases from diverse suppliers?

Purchasing schedules vary from company to company and product to product, so you will need to research timing with each individual company you choose to target. I will say, however, that selling to corporate America can be a very long process—lasting from several months to several years—but, as the following chapters will demonstrate, the rewards are well worth the wait. I encourage you to be aggressive, but also to be patient.

WHERE do I get started?

The best way to launch yourself into the world of supplier diversity is to become certified. The next chapter will show you how.

Success Story:
Terri L.C. Hornsby, President, TLC Adcentives LLC

Terri Hornsby is the embodiment of multi-tasking. Even as she demonstrates her competitive spirit—winning major contracts with multi-national firms—she continues her active leadership role in WBENC; its regional affiliate, Houston-based Women's Business Enterprise Alliance (WBEA); the National Association of Women Business Owners (NAWBO); and the Houston Minority Business Council, as well as other community organizations.

Terri founded TLC Adcentives LLC in 1995 and was certified as a Woman Business Enterprise in 1996. Her successful development from a home-based business into a commercial facility with warehouse capacity is based on her creativity and an exceptional business sense. She understands her clients' business objectives and reflects them well in interesting, quality promotional items.

According to Terri, "The best thing I ever did was get my certification as a minority- and woman-owned business through WBENC. Once I got active, I started to make the connections that really paved the way for my business to grow.

"I knew from the beginning that you have to do your best no matter how small a project may seem. After trying to get my foot in the door at Houston's huge energy companies for almost two years, I finally got my first call from Texaco. That first order for red star confetti with an invoice of $30.00 led to sales over $90,000 at the end of the year.

Shell Oil Company is another TLC client. In 2005, Shell began to narrow down their vendor base of promotional advertising firms. TLC was one of six firms selected out of over 150 firms to continue to work with Shell as a licensed vendor. According to Terri, this is particularly significant because the supplier diversity team stayed in the process to make sure that certified women and minorities did not get left out of the loop. This initiative tripled TLC's revenue with Shell in 2005.

"My deep satisfaction comes with watching this business grow—and with seeing the ideas I bring to clients take shape and help them achieve their objectives. This business is a combination of intuition, attention to detail and working with people. It is fantastic. I could not have made this happen if I did not love what I do."

Terri represents the interests of women business owners as a member of the WBENC National Forum and is active both on a local and national level. In 2002 she was a Salutee at WBENC's Salute to Women's Business Enterprises: The Enterprising Economy and received an NMSDC Regional Supplier of the Year award. She also serves on the Board of Directors for WBEA, the Houston Minority Business Council and NAWBO-Houston, where she served as president from 2002-2003. In 2004-2005, she served as a director-at-large for the national board of NAWBO. And in 2004, Terri received the 2004 Supplier of the Year award from the Houston Minority Business Council, thanks to a nomination from Shell Oil Company.

TLC's current client list includes the following corporations: Baker Hughes, Brown & Root/Halliburton, Chevron, Citgo, ConocoPhillips, Equilon Enterprises LLC, Equiva Services LLC, Guaranty Bank, HP, Houston Independent School District, Lubrizol, Marathon Oil Company, Motiva, Shell Oil Company and Toshiba International.

Chapter Two

Becoming Certified

"Since becoming certified, as much as 50 percent of my business has come through this channel."
- Debbie Faraone, president, The Elements, Inc.

The History of Certification

Supplier diversity officially entered the American business landscape in 1968 when the United States Small Business Administration (SBA) established a program to channel some government purchases to "disadvantaged" owners of small businesses. The following year, a presidential order established the Office of Minority Business Enterprise within the U.S. Department of Commerce to oversee this initiative.

In 1972, the National Minority Supplier Development Council (NMSDC) was founded to certify businesses as minority-owned. Many private sector supplier diversity programs were, in fact, originally created to identify minority-owned businesses and only later added women to the list of eligible companies. Part of the problem was the lack of a nationally recognized certification for women business enterprises, a void that WBENC filled with our creation of WBE certification in 1997. Today, WBENC certification is widely accepted and just as widely respected for its rigorous standards and consistent procedures.

Certification organizations such as WBENC and NMSDC provide corporations with a way to verify that companies qualify for their supplier diversity programs as 51 percent owned, managed and controlled by a woman or minority. Many local, regional and national government agencies also provide certification, as do a few smaller women and minority certification organizations. As mentioned earlier, certification is by no means a guarantee of a corporate contract, but it is a necessary first step to the supplier diversity opportunity.

Can certification be a complicated and time-consuming process? Yes, sometimes. Becoming certified is by no means easy, but this is one of the reasons corporations respect the qualification so deeply, and why supplier diversity professionals are so committed to helping certified businesses succeed. They know that a business owner who has successfully completed the demanding certification process is motivated, organized and ambitious.

Additionally, many certified businesses report that they learned invaluable information about themselves, their businesses and the supplier diversity marketplace while navigating the certification process.

Now it is your turn to get started.

Certification: A $1 million idea!

According to a 2004 study by the Center for Women's Business Research, woman-owned $1 million firms are nearly two and-a-half times as likely as other woman-owned businesses to be certified as a WBE.[iv]

The Steps to Certification

Step One: Learn the requirements for various certifications and decide which one is right for you.
Approximate Time: 1-2 weeks

There are four major criteria for certification by WBENC as a WBE. Review this list and be sure you are a qualified applicant before you begin the process:

- At least 51 percent ownership by a woman or women
- Proof of effective management of the business (operating position, bylaws, hire-fire and other decision-making roles)
- Control of the business as evidenced by signature authority on loans, leases and contracts
- U.S. Citizenship (WBENC, but not all certifying agencies, also provides certification to those able to verify U.S. Resident Alien Status)

For MBE certification, the NMSDC requires:

- "A for-profit enterprise, regardless of size, physically located in the United States or its trust territories, which is owned, operated and controlled by minority group members. Minority group members are United States citizens who are Asian-Indian, Asian-Pacific, Black, Hispanic or Native American. Ownership by minority individuals means the business is at least 51 percent owned by such individuals or, in the case of a publicly owned business, at least 51 percent of the stock is owned by one or more such individuals. Further, the management and daily operations are controlled by those minority group members."[v]

Federal government certifications also include requirements that your business meets certain size standards and that you fall under certain ceilings of personal net worth. Some government certifications still require proof that you are "disadvantaged." To meet this particular criterion, you must establish that you have been discriminated against economically and socially. If you are a member of certain ethnic minorities detailed in Chapter One, you are considered to be included in a "presumed class" and automatically meet those criteria. Non-minority women must make an individual case of societal discrimination by putting forward documentation on such experiences as the denial of credit, exclusion from educational opportunities or discriminatory hiring practices.

FAQ: Should I apply for more than one certification?

A: By all means! While it takes time and effort to apply for multiple certifications, you will increase your exposure to corporate and government contracts by applying for all of the certifications for which you are eligible. Some customers will even insist that you have a specific certification for their industry or region. As you have learned already, the most common national certifications include WBENC (for women business enterprises), NMSDC (for minority business enterprises) and various government certifications for all of the categories listed in Chapter One.

Leslie Saunders, WBENC-certified CEO of Leslie Saunders Insurance and Marketing, currently holds over 80 certifications. One of Leslie's early customers was Budget Rent-A-Car, which requested that she acquire local certification to fulfill their government airport contracts. Budget began to send her applications from other airport cities across the country, each of which required its own certification. Leslie hired a college intern whose entire job consisted of sorting through the certification process and assembling each application. The student organized it all and Leslie's business started getting certified—and getting business—all over the country.

While some of these individual certifications have now consolidated into regional certifications, Leslie still maintains her dozens and dozens of certifications in addition to her WBENC certification. "I hope I live to see the day when I will need only one national certification—WBENC—that is accepted everywhere!" she says.

Step Two: Visit the website of the organization(s) providing the certification(s) for which you plan to apply.

WBENC certification begins online at *www.wbenc.org*. I will use it as a model for navigating the online application process, but you will find that other certifications such as NMSDC's (available at *www.nmsdcus.org*) are quite similar.

Below is a graphic of the first page of WBENC's online certification form. Step one on the web is to set yourself up with a user account. This is quite similar to many other popular Internet sites such as eBay, Amazon.com or Yahoo.com. This account name and password will serve you throughout the online certification process and will allow you to log in and out as you work on the application.

Rest assured that no one expects you to complete your certification application all in one sitting. However, your application must be completed and submitted online within 90 days after you begin the application process. If your application has not been submitted within that time frame, the entire file will be deleted and you will need to start a new one. You will, however, receive reminder notifications to finish your application during this 90-day period.

WBENC
Password Registration

Please enter the requested information below. Your e-mail address and password will be used to identify you when you access your company's WBENC application. Upon the completion of this form, you will receive an e-mail that you can use to verify your password. If you do not receive an e-mail, complete the password registration process again and make sure your e-mail address was entered correctly.

Please keep your password for future updates to your WBENC application.

Required Fields marked with an asterisk(*)

* **Enter your e-mail address:**

Required * You must enter a valid e-mail address

* **Password:**   (Between 6 and 16 characters)

* **Retype your Password:**

* **Enter a hint to help you remember your password:**

Your Information

* **First Name:**

* **Last Name:**

* **Title:**

* **Phone Number:**

* **Company Name:**

You must enter a company name

Step Three: Meet your local partner organization.

Your online WBENC application will be assigned to a partner organization or WBOP (Women's Business Organization Partner) for processing (See Appendix B for a full list of WBOPs). When you have electronically submitted your application, you will be notified immediately by e-mail providing the name of the WBENC regional affiliate that will process your application and the fee for certification. Note that fees may vary from organization to organization, but will not exceed $350.

You will be required to print out your application (be certain to keep a copy for your own files—it will be useful when you apply for additional certifications from other entities). You will also need to attach the required documents, such as tax returns, bank signature cards and proof of citizenship (see the text box in this section). You will find a comprehensive list of these supporting documents at the website and you should review it before you begin the application process. Once you have compiled a complete application package, you must sign an affidavit and have that notarized, then send the notarized affidavit, copy of the application, required documentation and your check to the organization listed in the e-mail notification.

Take special care to make certain your application is complete when submitted. Missing documents are the single biggest factor in delays in the certification process.

The program managers at each WBOP are experts in the certification process. Be sure to access their expertise if you have any questions or problems. These people will also become excellent advisors after you receive your certification, as you navigate the supplier diversity process.

If you are a minority business owner seeking MBE certification, you should contact one of the National Minority Supplier Development Council's 39 affiliated regional councils and follow a similar process.

Step Four: Put it all together.

Depending on size of your business, you may need to contact your accountant and/or lawyer to obtain some of the necessary application documents that are referenced above. Most sole proprietors and Subchapter "S" Corporations find that they have the required documents in their normal business files. The longer you have been in business and the more complicated your business structure (if any of the ownership resides in trusts, for example) the more complicated the application and the process.

Liz Cullen, regional director of the Women Presidents' Educational Organization, always reminds WBE applicants to consider their application as a marketing document. "Think about how you want to describe your business and yourself as the CEO," she advises. "Carefully explain exactly what your company does. Check your spelling and grammar before you submit. Do not cut corners! Your application profile will become your online WBE profile when you receive your certification, so you should have a marketing mindset from minute one."

For a list of mandatory supporting documents for WBE application, see Appendix C.

FAQ: What are the biggest mistakes made by certification applicants?

A: Dr. Marsha Firestone, Ph.D., president, and Liz Cullen, regional director, of the Women Presidents' Educational Organization, a WBENC partner organization, point out five potential pitfalls:

- **Submitting an incomplete application** – Follow directions! If you neglect to answer certain application questions or forget to include required documents, the processing of your application will take extra time.
- **Waiting until the last minute** – There is no way to speed up the certification process, so, if a company has requested you become certified in order to do business with them, be

sure to give yourself enough time to complete the process. No applications are expedited, no matter what.

- **Not knowing your company's bylaws** – Liz says that she is often surprised how many women business owners do not understand their own bylaws. According to Liz and Marsha, sometimes the legal documents do not support the woman's claim that they run their company. "They go to an attorney, usually a person who has no experience with certification and think the cookie cutter bylaws will suffice. They end up creating bylaws that often favor the men in the company," Marsha says. "When it comes to certification, this can lead to a denial. Bylaws must state that all authority is with the woman, even if this harms some of the male egos in your company!"

- **Underpaying yourself** – Not getting paid what you deserve not only hurts your bank account, but it also hurts your WBE certification application. If you own, operate and control your business, your compensation should reflect that. The WPEO can cite examples of several businesses where a woman CEO hired her husband to work in the business and paid him more, perhaps to protect his ego or due to questionable financial advice. This raises a red flag with the certification committee as to who is really running the business. Do not let this happen to you—pay yourself like you are the boss, because you are!

- **Giving up independence** – Many women business owners have a male co-owner or stockholder on whom they rely for advice and information. It is fine to have advisors, but you must fully understand (and demonstrate your understanding of) the finances and operations of your business in order to become certified. As stated in WBENC Standards & Procedures, a WBE cannot have "substantial reliance upon finances and resources of males." If you feel intimidated by issues such as financial statements, take the time to educate yourself now—as your company grows larger, financial management issues will only become more complicated and more important. Do not depend solely on someone else to understand them for you.

Step Five: Review of application.
Approximate Time: 60-90 days from submission of a complete application.

Once you have submitted your complete application and paid the fee, the staff at the affiliate organization will review your file and contact you if there are missing documents. They may identify special issues that arise in the review of the application and provide a summary to the certification review committee.

A committee consisting of at least five businesspeople in your region will review your application. They each sign a non-disclosure confidentiality agreement before reviewing your file. The majority of the committee will be composed of representatives from corporations or public entities, and the remainder will be WBEs or representatives of community-based organizations with a related purpose. Most committees include an attorney and a Certified Public Accountant. For WBENC, all committee members undergo detailed training that is provided either by WBENC staff or program managers who have undergone WBENC's "Train the Trainer" conditioning. Rest assured that competitive businesses are never allowed access to your documentation, review or discussion, and WBENC's standards require that all reviewers sign confidentiality agreements.

Note that the committee only makes a recommendation on approval or denial. For WBENC certification, the WBOP Executive Director renders the final decision.

Step Six: Site visit.

After the committee has reviewed your complete application, a site visit will be arranged. You must be present at the site visit so that any questions that have arisen during the review process can be answered.

In the case of WBENC, the site visit is prescheduled with the woman business owner. The site visit reviewer will ask for clarification on any issues in question from the file review. They will ask for an overview of the business and operations in order to get a feel as to how the company operates. They will also request a tour of the facilities—but do not worry or clean too much. Certification is not a neatness contest!

Step Seven: Results.

You will be notified in writing within seven business days of your site visit if you are certified OR denied. When you are approved as a WBE, WBENC provides an explanation of your certification, which includes the description and Standard Industrial Classification (SIC) Code(s) and the North American Industrial Classification System (NAICS) Code(s) indicating the functional mission of the business.

Remember that your certification must be renewed annually, although site visits are conducted every other year at a minimum. You will be notified electronically 90 days prior to your expiration date to provide sufficient time to complete the renewal application. However, keep track of your renewal date, because recertification is the WBE's responsibility.

Off and Running!

When your WBENC partner organization or NMSDC council has approved your certification, you will have the privilege of being listed in your certifying organization's database.

WBEs will be given an online profile on WBENCLink, the

WBENC database of certified WBEs. You will also automatically be added to the listservs *WEBuy@wbenc.org* (offering contract opportunities for certified WBEs) and *WBENC-Discuss@wbenc.org* (a forum to discuss issues with other certified WBEs and learn of meetings, conferences, executive education and other programs). All of this is a sign that you are now a member of the exclusive club of women business owners who "get it" and want to "get" new contracts!

MBEs newly certified by the NMSDC are listed in the regional council's Minority Supplier Directory and in the NMSDC national database called the Minority Business Information System (MBISYS), to which all of the NMSDC's national corporate members have direct access. Like WBENC, the NMSDC offers educational seminars, training and technical assistance, executive education, business fairs, conferences and other network opportunities for certified suppliers.

While all of the above will take place automatically, certification should act as a starter pistol for you. You should *immediately* begin using your certification as a marketing tool. For openers:

- Add your certification to all of your marketing materials, including your business cards, stationery, website and letterhead. The next chapter provides much more detail about the importance of marketing yourself as a certified business and displaying appropriate certification logos and seals. You can access guidelines for use of the member seal at WBENCLink once you have been certified.
- Immediately contact your local WBENC and/or NMSDC affiliate to start building relationships in the certified community. At this point, you may ask to be matched with a mentor who can help you through the process of marketing yourself to large corporations as a newly certified business.

Once you have determined which companies you would like to target based on your earlier research, you must register on each of their supplier diversity websites. According to WBENC's 2003 *Access to Markets Survey*, almost all (95 percent) of the corporations with strong supplier diversity programs have a list or database of women and minority enterprise suppliers available to all company buyers.

The bad news is that most corporations have their own individual websites and you will have to register on each and every one of them. This is a good project for your administrative assistant or an intern. Once you have pulled together your information for your WBENC or NMSDC certification application, the data fields for the corporate registrations will be a snap. I am always surprised when I hear business owners complain about the "burden" of registering on many data bases rather than thanking the corporations for the opportunity to register, and for their effort to make that registration so accessible. We forget how much more annoying it is to find the right phone number in the company, wait on hold or to have a call returned and then wait for an application to be mailed. With online registrations the access is immediate, the accuracy of the information depends on your own input and there is no middleman to lose or misfile your application.

FAQ: What if my certification is denied?

A: Some people who apply for WBENC certification do so with the honest belief that they meet the criteria. They describe themselves to friends and relatives as such and believe in their heart of hearts that they are a woman business owner. What they do not understand is that "woman-owned business" is not synonymous with "certified Woman Business Enterprise (WBE)." They may be a 50/50 partner with a husband, male friend or male family member. That does not meet the test. They may hold the largest percent of ownership of a business, but if their ownership along with that of other women owners does not total 51 percent of the voting stock, they do not qualify. Remember, WBENC does not consider community property laws, so joint ownership with a male is not counted.

Denial does not always mean the end of the certification process. Sometimes documents such as bylaws are not clear or actually misstate the control of their company, as explained in the "Mistakes to Avoid" box in this chapter. If your application is denied, the reason for that denial will be included in your notification letter. If the reasons for denial are accurate, you can still market to corporations, just not through the supplier diversity program and not as a WBE. If you believe that your documentation has been misinterpreted, contact the partner organization and file an "appeal." Your denial may help you develop a good relationship with your local partner organization, as they can coach and counsel you on how to restructure, or perhaps re-explain, your business to qualify for certification.

Success Story: Nancy Connolly, CEO, Lasertone

Nancy Connolly, CEO of Lasertone, shunned "women only" groups for the first ten years she owned her own business, and she was cynical about state certification after attending a workshop and meeting people who were involved in their companies in name only. As her own company grew, Nancy eventually looked into WBENC. "After hearing Susan Bari speak at a corporate meeting, I realized how each regional affiliate meshed with the national program and I immediately saw value. When I experienced the thorough application process and site visit, I knew this was the real deal," she says.

Upon receiving her WBENC certification, Nancy immediately made herself visible through her presence at WBENC events and meetings. "Certification and my relationship with WBENC and its affiliates have opened significant doors for me," Nancy says. "It has given me the opportunity to have meetings with many Fortune 500 companies to whom I might not have had access."

Once skeptical of certification and affiliation with women's organizations, Nancy is now one of WBENC's biggest supporters. To celebrate Lasertone's 15th year in business, Nancy's company donated $15,000 to its local WBENC affiliate, the Center for Women and Enterprise in Boston, to help other growing WBEs achieve success and remains a board member.

According to Nancy, the most rewarding thing she has been able to do is to live the best practices of supplier diversity by implementing a program at Lasertone. Her program has been very successful, achieving five percent diversity spend in 2002, 8 percent in 2003, ultimately reaching 10 percent in 2004 with contracts totaling over a million dollars! As you can see, opportunities abound for certified businesses, not only with Fortune 500 corporations, but also with other certified WBEs. In Nancy's words, "We need to practice what we preach and help other women businesses grow."

In 2005, Nancy founded Smart Page Technologies, a document management consulting company. She will apply the best practices from Lasertone to her new company. "Diversity is not typically a major consideration when high-end consulting services are being considered for an organization," says Nancy. "As with any contract, we will earn our business based on merit and value, and continue to educate our customers as to the value of supporting diversity in their supply chain."

Chapter Three

Catching the Big Fish: Marketing

Let us deviate from the topic of supplier diversity for a moment and talk about fishing. Yes, fishing. Picture yourself as an ambitious and successful fisherwoman or fisherman, wanting to rise to the next level and catch the fabled "big fish." How would you go about doing this?

First, you would need to obtain a fishing license. Next, you would learn where the big fish live, and when they are in season. Then it would be a good idea to research what the fish like to eat so you can offer the most attractive bait. Finally, you would sit in your home and wait for the fish to swim up to your doorstep.

Huh?

Of course you would not wait for the fish to swim to your doorstep. Most likely you would get up at 5:00 a.m. and drive to the exact spot where the fish live, carrying all of your equipment and angling expertise with you. You would go back day after day, week after week, learning the patterns and idiosyncrasies of the fish. And eventually, the combination of hard work, knowledge, time and patience, would, you hope, result in snaring that big fish.

I use the fishing metaphor because I am constantly surprised at how many women and minority business owners work so hard to acquire a "fishing license" (certification), and then sit and wait for the "big fish" (corporate buyers) to come knocking on their doors for business.

Certification is *only a tool*. Becoming certified opens an

extraordinary opportunity for your business, but, as I have said before and will no doubt say again, certification does not guarantee that you will win a single corporate contract. Virtually every GME and supplier diversity professional I surveyed for this book said that the biggest mistake made by business owners is to assume certification is all they need to win business from corporate America. This could not be more wrong. Certification is like a gym membership—you will not see any benefits unless you use it.

The Eleven Commandments of GME Marketing

Certification must be accompanied by marketing. You need a strategic, multi-faceted, long-term marketing plan if you want to do business with the largest companies in America. As a successful business owner, you are likely to be quite familiar with many of the broad concepts in this chapter. Yet, I urge you to approach your supplier diversity marketing efforts with a new set of eyes and to remember that you are never "done" marketing. As the race car driver Mario Andretti once said, "If everything seems under control, you're just not going fast enough."

While you will rely on many of the marketing methods you have already employed to start and grow your business, you will need to alter many of your strategies to compete in the supplier diversity marketplace. The good news is that many GMEs have ridden this path before you, learning many valuable lessons that can make your path easier. Their wisdom—and warnings—appear throughout this chapter's list of eleven "marketing commandments" for doing business through the supplier diversity door to opportunity.

WBENC's 2003 *Access to Markets Survey* found that the top challenge to successfully selling to large corporations cited by women entrepreneurs was: *learning about opportunities.* The good news is that you can take steps to maximize your chances of learning about opportunities. As the first commandment on market research will demonstrate, you need to be proactive about researching opportunities through the Internet, associations, supplier diversity contacts and your WBE colleagues and competitors. Knowledge truly is power, and you need to have it in spades to succeed as a supplier to corporate America.

1. Know thy market.

There is only one place to start your strategic marketing planning: market research about potential customers. You must learn as much as you possibly can about your new corporate customer base. Many newly certified businesses have made the mistake of targeting their marketing efforts to corporations that do not even purchase what they produce or the service provided!

One of the advantages of contacting a corporate supplier diversity department is the large amount of information you can gather about your corporate customers. There is absolutely no excuse for ignorance. Besides the company's own website and publications, you can find an enormous amount of information in major newspapers, magazines and trade association publications. Supplier diversity contacts can provide additional insight and help you to target your approach within his or her company.

You should never contact a company without knowing as much as you can about what they purchase, when they purchase it, how they like to be contacted and who the key players are. In our highly networked world, there is simply no excuse for lack of knowledge about a company.

How Important is Research? Let Me Count the Ways...

A variety of supplier diversity experts from diverse companies weigh in on the importance of researching your potential corporate customers:

"Be strategic in the corporations you target so you can align your capabilities with the requirements of the buying organization. When certified business owners research Chevron's needs before approaching us, their business case is often well-prepared and focused. A customized proposal that recognizes our supply chain needs is the best marketing tool for anyone seeking business with our company."
   - Audrey Goins Brichi

Manager, Supplier Diversity/Small Business Program, Chevron
"The biggest mistake I see suppliers make is being unprepared—not doing their homework, researching our company, our customer base and the products and services we offer. It is false to believe that simply approaching us will result in business. Having a sound strategy is key to having a continuing opportunity to do business with us."
   - Bill Alcorn

Senior Vice President and Chief Procurement Officer, JCPenney
"One of the biggest mistakes a supplier can make is to expect supplier diversity professionals to educate him or her on the basics of our companies. Our time talking to you would be so much better spent discussing capabilities and contacts. So, understand the basics before you make that first call."
   - Ann Mullen
   Director, Supplier Diversity, Johnson & Johnson

"The most savvy and successful GMEs put great effort into learning about our company's business customs, culture and strategic needs. Then they use this knowledge as a component of their marketing strategy."
- Bruce Perkins
Vice President, Manager, Supplier Diversity & Business Development, Merrill Lynch

Here is a checklist of what you need to know about every corporate customer you plan to target with your marketing efforts. The more you know about your potential customers, the more you will be able to craft your marketing messages to address their needs and concerns—and the better you can avoid companies that are unlikely to work with you. Conduct this research for every corporation on your prospect list.

What does the company purchase?

This is the most basic information you need to know. Good supplier diversity websites, such as the UPS Supplier Diversity website featured in Appendix D, include a full list of their purchasing needs. Lists like UPS's do not serve as a guarantee that a company will purchase any of the listed products from a GME, but they provide guidance to suppliers about what products or services they will even consider procuring.

FAQ: What if my product or service is too unique to appear on a purchasing list, but I believe the corporation would be interested in what I provide?

A: This is where a visit to a national business fair, such as those sponsored by WBENC and the NMSDC or their affiliate organizations, is a good investment. Most major corporations will have representatives present with whom you can chat, either on the business fair floor or at the many networking sessions and content workshops that take place in conjunction with these events. Putting a face with a name will provide an enhanced opportunity for in-person, telephone or e-mail communication. (See Chapter Four for more information on business and trade fairs.)

For example, Pam Moore, president of Ice Tubes, Inc., produces a unique product that she began supplying to Wal-Mart under the company's local purchase program. She made her first national shipment the week of a national WBENC event in Chicago. At the event, she shared a lunch table with Excell LaFayette, director, and Mary Couchman, manager, of Wal-Mart Supplier Development. This face-to-face experience helped Pam build a stronger relationship and develop more support within the large company.

What is Pam's product? Plastic ice tubes for freezing water to insert into sports bottles. That certainly does not appear on "What We Buy" websites, but the president of Ice Tubes, Inc. believed in her product and developed the right relationships to make her business successful.

If appropriate, you might also send a product sample and ask for a critique from a supplier diversity executive with whom you have a good relationship. One WBE built a prototype instrument (at her own expense) to demonstrate that her company could handle a highly technical piece of business. She reviewed it with her customer, Johnson & Johnson. This extra effort impressed the buyers and won the WBE an even larger contract than she had before.

When do they purchase?

Gwendolyn F. Turner, manager of supplier diversity at Pfizer, says she hears the "when" question frequently. This information appears on the Pfizer website (as it does on most supplier diversity sites), but Gwen says it is actually the wrong question to ask. "Remember, we do not have opportunities every day, and if we do have opportunities, we often already have a preferred supplier in mind," she says. "So the better question is: What can you do to market yourself internally at a company to find out about opportunities when they do arise, and to become a preferred supplier yourself?"

In addition to heeding Gwen's wise advice, remember that, in general, corporate purchasing may not take place according to the same schedule or quantity allotment you may be accustomed to with smaller customers. In fact, a retail store like Macy's may purchase Christmas stock nine to twelve months in advance! Be sure to include timing in your company research, as it will become important later when you think about matching your production and distribution processes to your corporate customers' timetables.

How much do they purchase?

What is the average dollar amount spent on purchases in your niche? Is your point-of-sale price higher or lower than that of the company's existing suppliers? What is each company's current usage of your type of product or service offering, and is that usage likely to increase or decrease? How much do they buy at a time?

What department is responsible for purchasing your product or service?

While the supplier diversity department will be your entry point, it is important to learn as much as possible about the actual division(s) of the corporation that will make the final decision about your product. Your supplier diversity contacts will help lead you through the corporate maze, but even they may not know about *all* potential opportunities for your products or services. Be creative, resourceful and patient—diligently research the companies you are targeting and listen to what they tell you about their business needs across the corporation.

The answers are not always obvious, so you have to be open to a variety of possibilities. For example, Rebecca Boenigk, a certified WBE and CEO of Neutral Posture, Inc., wanted to market her ergonomic chairs to the gaming industry. Her natural thought was that companies would want to purchase the chairs for their casino floors. However, as Rebecca conducted her market research, she learned that there was an even larger market for her products: the back offices at casinos. Rebecca discovered that, for every table and chair you see at the casino, there are three times that number of chairs in the back offices where these businesses are run. If Rebecca had only pitched her chairs to the buyers responsible for furniture on casino floors, she would have missed an enormous opportunity.

To date, Neutral Posture has sold about $100,000 worth of chairs for the back offices of two casinos. "It is a very slow process," she admits, "but we are moving through it." To expand her reach even further, Rebecca is working on supplying chairs for casino hotel rooms as well.

While you are thinking creatively about where you might fit into a corporation, it is also okay to think small. After all, the small fish can often lead you to the bigger catches. Annette Taddeo, president and CEO of the translation company LanguageSpeak, Inc., began her relationship with Office Depot with what she describes as a "very small" contract. "But," she says, "I was able to build on that to the point that now we have a large contract with Office Depot, translating and maintaining their website in Spanish, in addition to working with other departments within the company. Also, the services offered to Office Depot have resulted in a lot of business with other corporations who learned about LanguageSpeak through our work with Office Depot." Annette adds that her business has grown by 100 percent in each of the past three years. She attributes more than half of that growth to her WBENC certification.

Think about how you might "start small" with some of your target prospects—perhaps offering a limited range of products or services, or serving a specific geographic area.

How do they purchase?

Become an expert in the administrative practices of your prospect companies. Does the company procure entirely online? Do they demand many face-to-face meetings? Do they require you to warehouse the product under contract and deliver "just in time"? If so, what are the additional costs to your company and what are the increased risks? If this is the case, you will want to think about including your ability to meet certain administrative or technological requirements in your marketing materials (see Chapter Six for more information on technology).

How is the company positioned now and into the future?

Pay close attention to industry trends related to the future of your products or services, as well as the future of the companies with which you would like to do business. Are there any timely, urgent issues you can address (remember the Y2K uproar)? Are there any major technological changes down the road that you can anticipate? (Think of all the typewriter suppliers who lost business when computers took over.) Are there rumors of mergers or acquisitions among particular companies? How are the company's finances? One successful WBE admits that, early on, she made the mistake of supplying companies that were near bankruptcy because she did not research their ability to pay. This resulted in some bad debt for her company. Do not let this happen to you.

Bill Moon, vice president of global sourcing at UPS, recommends that GMEs research the following information about prospect corporations:

- Goals and objectives
- Mission statement and business model
- Industry challenges—is the industry growing, on a plateau or in decline?
- Major competitors
- Are they currently gaining or losing market share, and why?

Remember, however, that any of the above information you discover does not prevent you from marketing to a particular company (in fact, some changes can be advantageous to suppliers), but should be part of your due diligence when creating a marketing strategy. As we will explore throughout this book, your job as a marketer is to tie *your* value proposition to the corporation's specific mission and goals. The most compelling sales pitches explain how *you* can solve a corporation's business challenges.

Joan Kerr, executive director, Supplier Diversity Program, AT&T, also points out that corporate business models and their associated goals, challenges and supplier opportunities are always subject to change. For example, many IT and telecom OEM (original equipment manufacturer) companies that used to be in the business of manufacturing are now completely outsourcing the manufacturing and warehousing of their products in order to focus exclusively on the research and development of new product offerings. Ten years ago this was unthinkable, but these industries' business models have shifted. This creates a vast opening for GMEs in the IT manufacturing sector. Can you benefit from a shift in the way corporations in your industry do business? Keep your finger on the pulse of your field to detect potential changes and opportunities.

An Important Note

In their handbook, *I'm Certified, Now What?*, Carol Dougal and Hedy Ratner of the Women's Business Development Center in Chicago remind certified businesses not to consider *all* corporations as their target market. You will be required to invest serious time and energy in following up with every corporation you contact by either filling out vendor application forms and/or making follow-up phone calls. Consider whether you have the staff to build relationships with hundreds of corporations. Be realistic!

Lynn Boccio, vice president, Strategic Business and Diversity Relations of Avis Rent A Car and Budget Rent A Car, concurs. "Do not use the 'shotgun' approach," she advises. "Target a reasonable number of corporations to market to, and then learn how to effectively follow up with your contact at the individual company and stay the course."

Spotlight: Helping Companies Reach New Markets

Annette Taddeo of LanguageSpeak is a firm believer in the importance of research in the marketing process. "I do a lot of research on the companies I think could use our services and then I specifically target companies I think I can help. For instance, if I learn that a company is starting to market to the U.S. Hispanic market and they have a budget to grow that customer base, then they are going to need my Spanish translation services—and of course I go after them!"

Do your products or services target a specific demographic? If so, seek out companies wanting to launch or expand business with that market. If you are not sure, you may consider attending an informational workshop on that particular market segment or hiring a consultant who can help you assess whether or not you are in a position to address their needs. For instance, Annette is currently advising fellow WBE Sharon Avent, president and CEO of Smead Manufacturing Co., on potential opportunities for her company to help corporate customers doing business in the Hispanic market.

2. Know thy competition.

In order to make your marketing message stand out to a corporate supplier diversity representative, you need to differentiate yourself from the crowd, a.k.a. your competitors.

You will want to find out:

Who are my primary competitors and are they doing business with any of the companies I plan to market to?

There are many ways to find this out. Networking in trade associations can provide information. Industry newsletters will sometimes include information on recently completed agreements. If your target company is a government contractor, they are required to list the names of their diverse subcontractors in their subcontracting plans. As discussed previously, the Internet offers a wealth of data. If the company is retail, you can visit a location to determine what they are buying and from whom. Do not forget the most obvious method—ask the buyer. They will often tell you directly.

Do research on both GME and non-GME competitors as you will likely be competing with both. And even if you are a small shop, learn who the "big players" are in your industry. You may want to borrow their tactics or connect with their leaders for advice, mentoring or strategic alliances (see Chapter Five for information about strategic alliances and Second Tier supplying opportunities). Do not forget that there may be Second Tier opportunities for you with a prime contractor.

What are the strengths and weaknesses of my competitors?

Do your best to collect competitors' ads and literature. Study them for information about strategy, product features and benefits. At the very least, familiarize yourself with the website of each competitor. When you are redesigning any of your marketing materials, look to your "competitor file" for ways to differentiate yourself. Ask: What opportunities can you find in the weaknesses of your competitors? Are you faster? Less expensive? More technologically advanced? When I was a manufacturers' representative, I would visit a retail outlet of each of the companies I called on before I made that first call. As I was already familiar with my competition from attending semi-annual trade shows, I could tell on the spot who they were currently buying from, the apparent age of the merchandise (which told me whether it was appropriate for their market or priced correctly), the pricing and mark down policies and the general taste of the buyer. That information allowed me to hone my pitch and close more business.

Competitive research needs to be part of your ongoing marketing strategy, even when you secure and begin to service corporate contracts. The supplier diversity marketplace, as is true of the entire business marketplace, is very competitive and you need to stay one step ahead of the game.

Once you have done your research on what your corporate customers need and what your competitors are lacking, it is time to show how your company is the perfect solution.

3. Know thyself.

All of your marketing messages should include information about your company's unique value proposition in the overall marketplace, and in the GME marketplace in particular. What will make you stand out to a supplier diversity representative or purchasing manager? Remember, with corporate customers it is just as important to market your capacity to do business with the big guys as it is to market your products or services.

Cheat Sheet: Defining Your Value Proposition

Consider these questions when defining your value proposition and developing marketing messages that will appeal to the companies you plan to approach:

- Do you have a highly specialized product or service that few companies offer?
- Can you offer a smaller or cheaper version of a particular product or service?
- Can you offer a fancier or more expensive version of a particular product or service?
- Do you offer a higher level of experience than your competitors?
- Are you geographically desirable?
- Do you have strong technological and administrative capabilities that prove your ability to work efficiently with a large corporate buyer?
- Are you more creative than your competitors?
- Are you faster than your competitors?
- Are you more cost effective than your competitors?
- Are you more flexible in terms of design modifications?
- Do you offer a broader catalogue of synergistic products?
- Does your financing structure offer greater flexibility in payment terms?
- Do you have compatible technologies?
- Are you registered with electronic commerce entities utilized by the client?

If you are a small business, be sure to promote the positive aspects of large corporations' doing business with you. As WBE Nikki Olyai of Innovision Technologies, Inc. points out, many corporations recognize and leverage the unique values that small businesses   provide, such as responsiveness, creativity, innovation, flexibility, service, customization and quality. While you might face challenges as a small business, you can do everything in your power to create the positive marketing messages that point out the strengths of your size.

4. Create new collateral around thy certification.

If you have it, flaunt it! No one will know you are a certified business unless you share the news. Upon receiving your certification, add the logo of the certifying organization to your business cards, website, letterhead, trade show booth and all other marketing materials. This "seal of approval" will be noticed by purchasers, competitors and potential networking contacts— and will work to your advantage. In addition to including your certification in marketing materials, I recommend including any industry or association affiliations as well. They all promote your credibility as a company poised to do business in major markets. If you have other certifications, such as ISO 9000, prominently list those as well.

- Will these changes and new materials cost money? Yes, but you really do have to spend money to make money. When you plan to do business with large, successful corporations, you will need to look the part. If you are unhappy with your current image, certification can act as an opportunity to update your company's look. But do not tinker too much with what has worked to make your business successful to this point. Creating certification-related marketing messages and materials should *complement* your existing image and branding, not necessarily replace it.
- Collateral materials are enormously important. As we all know, first impressions are crucial. Here are some additional tips gathered from WBENC-certified businesses:

- Put your certification front and center. This is a great tip for any certified business, but can be particularly helpful for young companies. Leonor McCall Rodriguez, president of Mira Promo, Inc. has found this strategy effective in marketing her relatively young Hispanic marketing agency and Latino Speakers Bureau. All of Mira Promo's brochures, publications and letters begin by stating that the company is a WBE-certified business and the WBENC seal appears on all correspondence. Leonor has found that this strategy gives corporate buyers confidence that, while her business may be relatively new, it will be around for a long time.

- Ask fellow certified businesses for recommendations of graphic artists, copywriters, web designers and other marketing professionals who can provide expert services. This is not the time for you to experiment with clip-art. Whenever possible, you may want to give your business to a fellow GME, and perhaps barter your services. You can post an RFP (request for proposal) or "sources sought" notice on *WEBuy@wbenc.org* to reach all of WBENC's certified businesses throughout the country. Send your request to *B2B@wbenc.org* and it will be posted for you. If you are WBENC-certified yourself, you can search WBENCLink, the Internet-accessible database of WBE firms.

- Produce separate business cards and marketing literature for each of your target market segments if they require different messages. For instance, you might want to create separate brochures for government and corporate clients, or business-to-business versus business-to-consumer audiences.

- Consider purchasing a memorable toll free phone number that relates to your business so your prospects can easily contact you. Could anyone forget Ukrainian egg artist, author and professional speaker Jane Pollak's former toll-free number, 877-EGG-LADY?

- Create low-cost focus groups. Test your new marketing materials on friends, staff members and other business people, particularly corporate executives. Do they feel your logo appears professional enough? Is your website clear and easy to navigate? Are there any mistakes or inconsistencies in your marketing pieces? Do not let a prospect be the first to alert you to a typo in the brochure of which you just printed 10,000 copies.

Spotlight: Think Big

Sometimes you have to think like the big guys to win contracts with them.

Nancy Connolly of Lasertone, who launched her recycled toner cartridge business with one partner and big dreams in 1989, made a conscious decision never to act like a small business.

"After one year, with just the two of us, we did $22,000 in sales. Rather than starting with small clients to build a base, as our competitors were doing, we went after the best company names as customers. We viewed the large competitors like HP and studied their strategy rather than emulating companies our own size. We dressed like we were IBM, we acted like we were IBM and if we could not do it first class, we would not do it. All the fledgling companies took business card size ads in local business journals, while we did quarter-page ads and made a full year's commitment to get better rates and placement. I did the creative on the ads and coerced the publications' design people into putting images into my design template. We were off and running. At that point we were a three million dollar company. We had immediate name recognition.

5. Take full advantage of thy online marketing opportunities.

As you have no doubt noticed, much of the business of

supplier diversity takes place online: company research, certification, database listings and more. This means a large proportion of your marketing efforts should also take place on the web.

Start with the easy stuff

Now that you are certified, you have the privilege of listing your business on many websites, databases and directories for purchasers. Take advantage of every easy opportunity to market your business! One caveat—be sure to proofread your directory listings and keep them updated with any changes in contact information, product offering or other news. Do not let your listings become stale. Keep a record of all of your postings for easy management.

In addition to the previously discussed acts of listing your certified business with WBENC or the NMSDC and your local affiliate of these organizations as well as the corporations with which you would like to do business, additional places to list your business include:

- Local Chambers of Commerce
- Industry trade associations
- The U.S. Government's Central Contractor Registration (*www.ccr.gov*)
- The Yellow Pages!

Create the highest quality website you can afford

Many supplier diversity professionals and purchasing managers will visit your website as part of the vetting process. Make sure that your site accurately reflects your brand, your competitive edge and your capacity to do business with large customers. If you are still living with a website your teenager designed in the early days of the Internet (you know who you are!), now is definitely the time to upgrade.

Here are additional suggestions from the most web-savvy

GMEs I know:

- If you have not already done so, obtain a memorable URL that is as close as possible to your business name. Be sure to acquire e-mail addresses with this URL as well. It is much more impressive and not expensive at all, to have an e-mail address of "Jane@JaneDoeEnterprises.com" rather than JaneDoeEnterprises@hotmail.com.

- On the topic of e-mail, create a "signature" to appear at the bottom of all e-mail messages you send. This signature should include your full contact information, logo, website URL (including an active link to click to your website) and of course, your certification. Online marketing experts also recommend adding an additional, customized line at the bottom of your signature: the tagline of your company, information about an upcoming event at which you are speaking, a new product launch or the name of a book or article you have recently written. On my own WBENC signature, I include our tag line—"Creating Opportunities...Recognizing Excellence"—and frequently add a sentence about an upcoming event.

- Do not be shy about using your e-mail signature to announce awards you have won (see the next section for advice on applying for awards) or honors you have received. I remember that Terry Neese, co-founder and former president of Women Impacting Public Policy (WIPP) had an e-mail signature announcing the fact that *Fortune* magazine named her the sixth most influential small businessperson in its 2003 list of "Power 30 on Capitol Hill."

- Mention your website address (URL) on ALL of your marketing materials—no exceptions!

- Make sure that all of your contact information is available and easy to find on your website, preferably on a standard "Contact Us" page. Do not make a prospective buyer search for a way to call you if he or she wants to meet you! On a regular basis, "Google" yourself and your company to see how your name comes up in searches for your product, service or company. If it is not coming up the way you believe it should, talk to your website designer about maximizing your search engine results.

- Consider paying "per click." Some companies invest big advertising dollars to make sure they show up on Google and other search engines. I first heard about this strategy at a NAWBO conference, where I met Sharon Newman, the head of Action Envelope & Printing Co., Inc. Sharon took over the company when her husband died suddenly in 1993 and brought her son into the company when he graduated from college in 2000. "It is such an advantage to have young blood in the business with new ideas," Sharon says of her son. Why? He encouraged her to grow the company's online business, setting up an e-commerce site. Sharon's son designed their first website himself, winning a grand total of one order its first month—a sale of eleven dollars. In the website's second month, they drew a few more orders, and then in the third month the site began to generate thousands of dollars in sales. "At that time we did not send people there, but we saw that it had potential," says Sharon.

Next, Sharon invested in a professionally designed site, and, she says, "It became clear that we had to push traffic." To do this, the company began "pay-per-click" advertising, where you bid a certain amount of money that you agree to pay if someone clicks on your URL (on Google, or other search engine websites). Sharon explains, "Only by bidding higher do you ensure you will be at the top of the list. You give them your credit card and they charge you each day. This has to be monitored hourly. That is because at any time one of your competitors can decide he or she wants to be number one and they can outbid you. My son manages that part of the business—he sits in front of the computer all day. If you type the word 'envelope' into Google, we will usually be number one, but never less than number two [in the list of advertised links]." This is absolutely true—I tried it!

This strategy is not cheap. According to Sharon, Action Envelope spent close to half a million dollars on pay-per-click advertising in 2005. But the investment pays off: Since Sharon took over the business in 1993 and devoted resources to e-commerce, Action Envelope's revenue, which had been declining due to the popularity of faxing and e-mail messaging, has increased ten-fold.

- Include all recent press releases, news articles, by-lined articles and other proof that you are "on the move" and recognized in your industry or community. Do not be shy about promoting any publicity you have received. No press release? Why not? Take every opportunity to write a press release. The word "press" is loosely used. You can send the release to local business journals and industry papers, but do not forget to send it to your customers and prospects as well.

Here are some examples of WBE press releases:

PRESS RELEASE

Casco is Certified as a Women's Business Enterprise by the Women's Business Enterprise National Council

CINCINNATI, OH (September 6, 2002) - Casco Manufacturing Solutions has been certified as a bona fide Women's Business Enterprise by the Women's Business Enterprise National Council (WBENC), an organization chartered to enhance and promote procurement opportunities for woman-owned businesses.

With the WBE certification, Casco also is enrolled in the Women's Business Enterprise Council—Southeast, a regional organization of the WBENC.

Casco, a privately held, contract manufacturer of commercially sewn and sealed products for OEM healthcare and consumer products companies, is led by Melissa Mangold. Its headquarters and plant are in Camp Washington. According to a recent Cincinnati Business Courier newspaper ranking, Casco is the fourth largest woman-owned business in the Greater Cincinnati region.

WBENC, based in Washington, D.C., fosters diversity in business through programs and policies designed to expand opportunities and eliminate barriers in the marketplace for women business owners.

Through its regional organizations, WBENC certifies businesses as woman-owned, managed and controlled, then provides information about those companies to purchasing managers of corporate partners through an Internet database.

WBE certifications are accepted by more than 500 major U.S. corporations, opening access to purchasing agents of Fortune 1000 companies across the country.

In business for more than 40 years, Casco is an ISO 9001 registered contract manufacturer specializing in custom services for U.S. healthcare companies and various consumer product companies. Services include engineering and design assistance, prototyping, complex sonic and radio frequency welding, project management and job costing.

To find out more, contact Casco Manufacturing Solutions, visit *www.cascosolutions.com*.

For more information about WBENC certification, visit *www.wbenc.org*.

#

PRESS RELEASE

**City Lights Electrical Co., Inc. Founder and CEO Named
2003 Entrepreneurial Success Winner for Massachusetts
and New England**

Boston, MA- City Lights Electrical Co., Inc., the premier union electrical contractor in the New England area, has been named the U.S. Small Business Administration's 2003 Entrepreneurial Success Winner for Massachusetts and New England; and is now being considered for the 2003 National Award in Washington, D.C.

"This is a well-deserved and distinct honor and it reflects the hard work and perseverance you have shown in growing your business. Your dedication to the success of your business, to the welfare of your employees, to the satisfaction of your customers, and your commitment to the community at large are exemplary and we congratulate you," states Elaine Guiney, Massachusetts Director of the U.S. Small Business Administration, in speaking of Maryanne Cataldo, president and founder of City Lights Electrical Co., Inc.

City Lights Electrical Co., Inc. received the award during the Small Business Week celebration.

# # #

PRESS RELEASE
Chester Community Charter School and Bosha Design Launch a New Website

Drexel Hill, PA (February 25, 2004) - The Chester Community Charter School (CCCS), of Chester, PA, and Bosha Design, Inc., of Drexel Hill, are excited to announce the launch of CCCS new website that will link the school's students, teachers, parents, and community (*www.chestercommunity-charter.org*).

The new website is informational and innovative. In addition to providing an overview of the school, it will also serve as a portal through which teachers will communicate with students and parents. A sophisticated content management system will give teachers the ability to develop and maintain their own personalized web pages. They will use these pages to inform students and parents about upcoming events, lesson plans, future projects, and to keep parents and guardians up-to-date with classroom activities.

Students will also have access to the content management system. They will be able to create their own web pages, complete with custom colors and fonts. They will be able to upload pictures, class projects, and some of their favorite things. Parents and students can access a wealth of information such as: what is being served in the cafeteria, the latest school news, information about teachers, and students' progress and projects.

CCCS is an elementary school in its sixth year of operation. It is dedicated to empowering students as learners through the development of a learning community. Starting with an initial enrollment of 97 students, it now has an enrollment of 1,004.

"The Internet presence of CCCS via our newly designed website creates a dynamic process whereby we can communicate with parents, as well as the local and the global community," according to a statement from Peter M. Idstein, CAO, and Dr.

Melvyn Burroughs, Principal. "Teachers and parents will have immediate access through email, and CCCS families will find updated information about school events, parent meetings and classroom assignments. This is our school's entry into the world of global communications."

In addition to the school's website, Bosha Design created collateral materials to support the launch, including an informative brochure about the school and a postcard announcement of the site launch. Balloons, pens, and magnets were also produced, featuring the new CCCS mascot that was developed and created by Bosha Design.

Founded in 1986, Bosha Design sets itself apart by providing unmatched creativity with unparalleled service to achieve client objectives. Bosha Design's creative team possesses solid agency, marketing and technical experience, from strategy and implementation to project management.

Barbara Bosha is a member of the American Institute of Graphic Arts (AIGA), International Association of Business Communicators (IABC) and Association for Women in Communications (AWC). The Women's Business Enterprise National Council has certified Bosha Design, Inc., as a Woman Business Enterprise (WBE).

—

Contact:
Barbara Bosha
barb@boshadesign.com
www.boshadesign.com

# # #

- Create an area of your website specifically for customer and potential customers. This area can provide tailored content so your valued clients can immediately find the information that is relevant to their needs. Do not make your clients "surf" around your site to find the information they need.
- Include downloadable information documents on your site (such as that press release you just created), preferably in PDF format. This will allow prospective customers and others to read any position papers, annual reports or other documents that may be too long or text-heavy to include as web pages. This can be a particularly good strategy for owners of companies that produce complicated products.

Even if your product or service is not complicated, you should always have your graphic design firm provide you with PDF versions of any new brochures or reports. PDFs are good for two reasons: Most people have the software (Adobe Acrobat) to open the files, and PDF files cannot be altered when downloaded from your website (as Word or Power Point files can).

- Update your site frequently (at least once a month) with "news flashes" on the home page, new client listings, new testimonials or other fresh content. No one returns to a site that seems stagnant or neglected. Be certain to mention if you are a speaker or a panelist for a business conference or community event. When Christine Bierman, CEO and founder of Colt Safety, Fire & Rescue was invited to speak at a small business event with President George W. Bush, she posted the announcement on the home page of her company's website with a direct link to the accompanying article on the website of—you guessed it—The White House. She also includes a direct link to WBENC in her e-mail signature and on her website.

6. Market thyself as an expert.

Corporate purchasers are interested in the specifics of your business, but they are also very interested in you as the owner and operator of your business. Take advantage of opportunities to market yourself as the head of your company and as an industry leader. Some women, especially those of us "of a mature age," do not want to appear pushy (or learned at a young age that "the boys would not like it"), so we do not put ourselves up front. This is a mistake—you absolutely can be present and polite at the same time. In fact, the success of your business may depend on your ability to (politely and professionally) promote yourself as a business owner.

Create marketing materials about YOU.

Pay as much attention to the writing and editing of your professional bio as you do to the marketing copy promoting your business. Post your bio on your website and include it in marketing packages for potential customers. A professional, up-to-date headshot is essential as well. (While digital cameras are terrific to document the company picnic, rely on a professional to create your headshot.)

Speak at professional events.

Professional speaking is a great way to make yourself known in your industry. Contact your local WBOP, industry association, Chamber of Commerce, Rotary Club or other organization (see the Resource Guide in the back of this book for additional suggestions) to learn about opportunities to speak about important issues in your field or your local business community.

If you do not have the time or the desire to prepare a keynote address, seek out opportunities to speak on panels instead. Another option for the time-pressed (or nervous) is to speak virtually. Many organizations and businesses now host tele-classes (seminars by phone) or offer online educational opportunities featuring live chats with speakers. For instance, Office Depot's "Web Café" web seminar series (*www.officedepot.com/webcafe*) features women experts on various topics offering their knowledge and advice to women business owners.

Cheat Sheet: Speak Up!
Making the Most of Your Public Speaking

When you do speak, virtually or in-person, maximize the experience:

- Invite business partners, clients, potential customers, supplier diversity contacts and the press to attend your events. Although they may not come, people will certainly take note of your status as a professional expert "on the circuit."
- Promote the events at which you are speaking on your website.
- Ask someone to take photographs during your speech (digital, if possible). You can post these on your website or include them in press kits to show your expert status.
- Bring your own bio to provide to the person who will introduce you. Make sure you are presented the way you want to be.
- Discuss your certification in your remarks to show your credibility and increase your appeal to any potential corporate customers in the audience.
- Videotape your speeches so you can review your performance at a later date. If you cannot videotape your speech, audiotape yourself with a small handheld recorder.
- Bring plenty of business cards and other marketing materials to any event at which you speak. Leave your cards on a table or hand them to all attendees.
- Try to obtain a list of attendees at any speaking engagement so you can follow up with potential leads, or add attendees to your marketing database.

Write articles

There are hundreds of opportunities to write and publish expert articles. You can pitch articles as short as 500 words to your industry association newsletter, e-newsletter, website, magazine or other publication. Consider the business section of your local newspaper as well. At the very least, publish your articles on your own company's website. A by-lined article is a great indicator not only of your expert status, but also of your desire to share your views with other professionals in your field.

To maximize the marketing potential of your written pieces:

- Always send a thank you note to the editor who hired you to write for the publication. Keep these relationships strong so editors will keep your name on file and invite you to write more articles in the future.
- Post your written articles on your website and include reprints in any media kits or other marketing packages. WBE Nancy Michaels, president of Impression Impact suggests that you reprint any published articles in color (if the original article appeared that way) and on the highest quality paper stock available—no one is impressed by smudged photocopies.
- Cross market by writing a press release (and posting it prominently on your website) directing people to the article source. For basically the same amount of work you get double exposure! That way, if your client or prospect does not have time to read the article, they will at least get a pithy quote or key message digested in the press release.

Apply for awards.

Awards are important credentials that can help your marketing efforts. The next chapter offers advice on applying for awards given by associations to which you belong. WBENC and the NMSDC have awards programs, as do most local certification bodies. Additional places to look for award opportunities include: Chambers of Commerce, volunteer organizations, local and national newspapers and magazines, and university alumni associations. When you do win an award, be sure to send a press release to the media and your existing and potential customers to share the good news. Also add any awards to your professional bio and, of course, your website.

Conduct and promote original research.

Particularly if you produce a unique product or service, conduct surveys and research projects to educate your customers about your specialty. To gather information, marketing expert Joyce L. Bosc recommends including a postage-paid survey card with your brochures and other company literature that asks customers and potential customers for feedback that can help you develop relevant products and services.

Online surveys are an even easier, as well as inexpensive way to gather information about a topic of particular interest to you. At WBENC we use SurveyMonkey.com when we survey our membership, which markets itself as being able to enable *anyone* to create professional online surveys quickly and easily.

Once you have your research findings, develop a press release or article to announce your results to your customers, potential customers, the media and other relevant audiences in your industry. You might also incorporate targeted survey results into a new business pitch.

Be an industry resource.

Another smart way to demonstrate your expertise and stay top-of-mind with potential customers is to send frequent news articles and items of interest to your supplier diversity contacts. "I thought this might interest you…" at the top of a forwarded industry article you have read is a great way to keep in touch without being a pest. This type of simple, no-cost marketing technique is great for managing the long months of the corporate decision-making process. My stockbroker is really good at this, and hardly a day goes by without a PDF of an interesting article about a stock I already own or one he believes I might be interested in. The subject line of the e-mail is clear so I can decide instantaneously whether to read, delete or save. This method of communication is fast and inexpensive. If you set up "blast" lists that you want to send materials to, send the message to yourself and put the list in the "bcc" (blind carbon copy) line of the address so that each recipient sees only his or her own name and not the entire list.

To take this suggestion one step further, consider producing your own e-newsletter. There are many simple, low-cost e-newsletter software programs available nowadays. Why wait for an editor to publish you when you can do it yourself? If you do not have a talent for writing, outsource the newsletter to a professional writer (ideally a fellow certified business) who will collaborate with you on content. You can use an e-newsletter to provide updates on your company's activities, provide tips for your customers, and promote events at which you or your staff will be speaking.

When creating and writing an e-newsletter, experts advise:

- Be very careful to only send the e-newsletter to people who have "opted in" and agreed to receive it. Federal regulations are becoming very strict against "spam" e-mails. You must also have an "opt-out" option.
- Be consistent with your delivery frequency. E-newsletters that appear at regular intervals, such as bi-weekly or monthly, are most likely to become "must-reads" for the recipients. However, avoid sending e-newsletters too frequently or your readers will feel bombarded.
- HTML is recommended, but stay away from too many bells and whistles. These frustrate recipients with slower modem

speeds and can also distract from the text you are presenting.

- Everyone loves quick and easy statistics and tips that relate to the product or service universe so they are a good first line in your newsletter. People will open the letter just to get the quote, tip or fact of the month.

- Interview clients, association members, fellow GMEs and others for inclusion in your e-newsletter. This will provide additional expert contact and show your strong relationships in the business world. As an added bonus, if you feature them in your e-news, they are likely to return the favor and feature you.

- Include your contact information prominently on the e-mail, so readers can get in touch with you easily.

- Copyright your newsletter and display the "©" symbol. This is easy to do yourself and will protect your original work.

Volunteer.

Giving back is not only good for the soul, it is good for business. Terri McNally, CEO of Global Capital, Ltd. was the volunteer organizer for a silent auction that benefits the Women's Business Enterprise National Council. Her important efforts benefit us at WBENC and provide Terri with the opportunity to call corporations to ask for donations, introducing and promoting herself, her company and her leadership relationship with WBENC.

Nikki Olyai, of Innovision Technologies in Michigan, strengthened her relationship with her client, Ford Motor Company, by engaging Dr. Ray Jensen, Ford's former director, Supplier Diversity Development, in a mentoring program she leads at a Detroit inner city school. A few years later when Ray retired from Ford, Nikki hired him as her company's president!

7. Market thyself in person.

Event marketing is one of the most effective tools available to GMEs. Numerous trade shows and business fairs across the country exist for the sole purpose of marketing certified businesses to supplier diversity professionals.

The drawback to event marketing, of course, is the time and expense it takes for you and/or your staff to attend various events and represent your business. The rewards, however, can be instant, as some corporate representatives may visit your booth and invite you in for an appointment on the spot. Do not regard event participation as time away from your business; rather see it as moving your business to the conference location. In addition to meeting targeted or new contacts, you will learn up-to-date information from the show's producers and have an opportunity to investigate your competitors and potential alliance partners.

Consider event sponsorship as well. Sharon Avent, president and CEO of Smead Manufacturing Co., makes event sponsorship an important component of her marketing. To help maintain her excellent relationship with her client, Office Depot, Sharon's company sponsors Office Depot's annual Success Strategies for Businesswomen Conference. "This does not mean that we automatically get their business," Sharon explains. But her sponsorship shows her commitment to her client and gives her a strong presence at this prestigious event. When Roz Alford and Nancy Williams of ASAP Staffing learned that BellSouth, a large client, was co-chairing WBENC's Women in Business: Sharing the Vision conference in 2006, Roz and Nancy signed up as WBE co-chairs. While every GME cannot afford to sponsor a large conference, smaller companies should consider sponsoring local or regional events to receive exposure to a targeted audience.

For much more on event marketing advice, see the next chapter on networking.

8. Solicit and use thy endorsements.

Satisfied customers provide some of the best and most effective marketing messages available. Get in the habit of collecting endorsements—in the form of short testimonial blurbs or full-length letters—from happy customers, vendors, employees, partners and industry experts. Most people will be more than willing to support you. "May I have that in writing?" should be your response to compliments. Be sure to save all testimonials and thank you notes, whether hard copy or electronic, in an easily retrievable file labeled "Endorsements."

As you collect endorsements, use them strategically in your marketing materials. You might, for instance, include a full range of testimonials on your website to show the diversity of your client base, but include only corporate testimonials in a brochure or media kit targeting a Fortune 500 purchaser.

9. Do not be afraid to go back to thy well.

One of the best lessons I have learned from reading business guru Tom Peters' books is the effective marketing strategy of seeking and winning more and more business from the same company. As you build and refine your marketing messages, do not be afraid to return and "re-market" to companies who may have rejected your business in the past, or to expand your offering to a single customer. Remember that corporations are enormous entities with many nooks and crannies needing new products and services all the time.

Your new certification is the perfect moment in time to revisit a potential customer relationship from your past. Or, if you were already doing business with a particular company before you received your certification, your new status may help you expand that business. All of your fishing need not take place in uncharted waters.

10. Always make time to market.

I can hear the voices in your head: "I know marketing is so important," you are thinking. "But how can I find the time to do all of this time-consuming marketing when I barely have time to blink?"

Here are some additional tips from other overworked entrepreneurs on how to make time for marketing:

Attempt to engage in at least one marketing activity every single day. Marketing should appear on every "To Do" list you have.

Get your staff to help. If you do not have an employee (or several) dedicated to marketing you and your business, assign this responsibility to someone on your team. Or, if you would prefer, hire a marketing consultant (there are many in the WBENC database alone) to advise you. In either case, schedule regular meetings with your key staff where only marketing issues will be discussed.

Take your marketing advice in doses. Sign up for free e-newsletters on the subject of marketing and set aside 30 minutes per week to review the advice, tips and strategies in these publications. Or, sign up for one marketing seminar every quarter. With the growth in online learning, you may not even need to leave your desk for the class.

11. Networking is marketing.

Finally, remember that even the most exquisite marketing brochure in the world is no match for having a personal connection with a potential customer. Networking may be the most important piece of your marketing pie. It is so important, in fact, that it merits an entire chapter all its own. Read on.

Success Story: Julia Rhodes, President and CEO, KleenSlate Concepts

It is both funny and interesting how necessity, lack of resources, and a creative imagination can be combined to create a simple, yet successful, marketing tool.

In 2001, after inventing and receiving her patent for the KleenSlate Attachable Eraser for Dry Erase Markers, Julia Rhodes was preparing to launch the eraser at her first trade show.   Julia realized that, because she would be working the event alone, her presentation had to be simple.   Both of her hands would already be busy, holding the dry erase markers and showing the KleenSlate Eraser in action.

Coincidentally, Julia was also trying to decide what to wear to the trade show.   A light bulb appeared: Could she create an outfit that could become a walking whiteboard?   Online research yielded a peel-n-stick whiteboard product that she could apply to the little black dresses left over from Julia's days as a jazz singer.   She called upon the creativity of a friend, and together, they altered the dresses to create wearable whiteboard surfaces.   The large circular dots of peel-n-stick whiteboard turned her dresses into an eye-catching, 1960s "mod" look.   Add a pair of white go-go boots and people could not help but notice Julia and her product! Wearing the KleenSlate outfit freed her hands and enabled her to write on herself and then easily erase with the KleenSlate Eraser while providing an instantly memorable impression.

Now, when Julia demonstrates her KleenSlate products at trade shows and conventions, she often get the reaction, "Can I write on you?" or "What a great party idea!" Or, "Aha! I wondered why you were dressed like that!" Julia is happy for any approach that initiates conversation and allows her to talk about her product. When she does her follow-up after shows, she always receives instant recognition as well as a friendly reception when she identifies herself as "the whiteboard eraser gal."

This creative marketing tactic has helped Julia succeed, with corporate clients in particular. At a WBENC business fair, Julia met Robert McCormes-Ballou, director, Vendor Diversity for Office Depot.

Robert, intrigued by the product, connected Julia with his assistant, Shari Francis, to further advance the relationship. Shari and Julia then developed a working relationship, which ultimately led to an Office Depot sponsored ad featuring KleenSlate. As Julia says, "The door had opened and I stepped on through!"

By 2005, Julia had earned a write up in Entrepreneur magazine and numerous awards from the educational market, including the prestigious Teacher's Choice Award for new products. She even found herself on The Tonight Show with Jay Leno. "It must have been that white board dress that got the attention of the producers," Julia says. "I had just finished teaching a workshop for inventors at the Yankee Invention Exposition, walked out of the class and onto a set that was filming inventors for The Tonight Show. I waited my turn to audition, wrote 'Pick me Jay' on my dress and landed the spot."

Julia appeared on the commercial and website advertising The Tonight Show's "Invent Across America." When Jay asked the audience what they thought of the KleenSlate Eraser, Julia's product received applause and a thumbs up from the audience. "I had a lot of people call to say they saw the show, and it helped get the word out and sell more products," she reports. Julia Rhodes certainly caught the big fish!

Currently, customers can find KleenSlate Erasers at all 1,007 Office Depot retail stores as well as 1,748 Staples stores nationwide. Last year, Staples added the KleenSlate Erasers to their catalog and website, and in 2006 you will be able to find all her current products online with Office Depot. With the growing success of her company, Julia has been able to add new products, enter into the promotional products industry and continue to help aspiring inventors pursue their dreams.

According to Julia, "It is impossible to measure just how important a role that little whiteboard outfit played in the whole scheme of things, but I have absolutely no doubt it did not hurt. The outfit has continued to serve me in my marketing efforts and perhaps it has even given a new meaning to the phrase, 'dressing for success.'"

Chapter Four

Networking

To say that I am an enthusiastic proponent of networking is a bit of an understatement. My husband, Dick, jokes that whenever I enter a room I start a receiving line. Lindsey Pollak, my younger friend and collaborator on this book, is similarly fanatical. She says that her girlfriends used to laugh at her for chatting up women in bars—in order to network—rather than flirting with eligible guys. You may not be as keen on networking as Lindsey and I, but networking must be part of your skill set if you want to build a successful company.

Think you are too busy running your business to make time for networking? Think again. As the CEO of your company, getting your face "out there" is an important part of your position description.

Even if you feel content with the current direction of your business, networking exposes you to a whole new world of possibilities. Consistent networking led me to one of the most exciting opportunities of my career. In the early 1980s I held a Presidential appointment in the Reagan Administration as Director of the Institute of Museum Services. My main contact in the White House Office of Presidential Personnel was a woman named Maryann Urban. At one of the dozens of receptions I took the time to attend each month, I saw Maryann and went up to chat with her.

"What's new?" I asked.

Maryann responded to my simple question by confiding that she was moving to Pennsylvania in two weeks to be closer to her significant other.

"But Maryann," I said. "If you leave The White House, who will be my contact?"

"Would you like my job?" she replied.

The next day I received a call from her boss, Bob Tuttle, and a week later I was sitting at my new desk in the Old Executive Office Building with the title of associate director of presidential personnel. This huge career opportunity arose because I had built strong, trusting relationships and I had shown up: networking.

As an interesting side note, I ran into Maryann in Pennsylvania, where she still lives and is now married to that significant other, at a joint Department of Labor/White House conference for women business owners. This time Maryann approached me, and she shared the fact that she now runs her own business!

I could share dozens of other networking stories, as could many of my colleagues and friends. Much has been written and discussed about networking, yet I am often surprised at how few business owners possess a true grasp of how to network effectively. Networking must be fully integrated into the daily operations of your business, not considered an extracurricular activity. Trust me, the more you do it the easier and more rewarding it becomes. As this chapter will demonstrate, many successful GMEs landed their biggest corporate customers through—you guessed it—networking.

First, I will address some of the common misconceptions held by skeptical business owners:

- Networking *is not* attending unlimited luncheons to collect and distribute as many business cards as humanly possible.
- Networking *is not* joining 65 associations and never attending any events.
- Networking *is not* meeting people and telling them what *they* can do for *you.*

- Networking *is not* something to be dreaded!

Networking *is*, quite simply, the building and nurturing of professional relationships. Your network of contacts is one of your most valuable assets as a business owner. And remember, networking is not just about who you know; it is about who knows *you*. If you are new to the world of supplier diversity, you absolutely must network to make yourself known.

Woody Allen once said, "Eighty percent of success is showing up." I can personally attest to the validity of that statement. I travel quite a bit and try to attend the business fairs and conferences of WBENC's affiliate organizations and the many other business-focused groups with which we maintain cooperative relationships. Just as you market your company, I walk the floor of the shows introducing myself and WBENC or just saying hello to WBENC members and prospect companies. At one such event, I stopped by the Kellogg booth to say hello to Cathy Kutch, Kellogg's director of supplier diversity. I had met Cathy on many occasions and had "pitched" her on Kellogg's joining WBENC as a corporate member. Unexpectedly, she turned to me and said, "I see you at all of these supplier diversity events and appreciate the fact that you support other organizations." She then told me to send her an invoice for corporate membership.

This chapter offers the most effective networking activities for building your reputation and relationships in the particular world of supplier diversity. While many of the networking techniques in this chapter apply to any business owner, keep in mind that GMEs face special networking challenges and enjoy unique opportunities.

The biggest challenge to networking in this community is its size. While corporate America is big, the corporate supplier diversity community is not. Supplier diversity professionals are a tight-knit group and their numbers are relatively small, consisting of about 1,000 people across the country. This means that first impressions are important and less-than-stellar first impressions can be difficult to overcome.

I must say (and you will see from the valuable advice they share in this book) that just about everyone I have met in the supplier diversity community is both very kind and passionately dedicated to helping GMEs succeed. Supplier diversity professionals are your advocates—as you read in Chapter Two, it is their job to help you. However, the truth is that they are more likely to help you if you have built a relationship with them. We are all overworked and our time is always double booked, so the phone calls we return are the calls from people we have met, know about and want to talk to.

You may notice that the names of particular certified WBEs— such as Rebecca Boenigk, Nancy Connolly, Nancy Michaels, Leslie Saunders, Nikki Olyai and Annette Taddeo—appear frequently throughout this book. This is because these women *show up all the time.* I know their stories because they share their news with me and let me know how I can help them. They are also willing to offer their assistance whenever called upon to mentor a new WBE, volunteer, or donate time or money to a WBENC initiative.

How do you make yourself as known and appreciated as these women? Show up! You MUST attend business fairs, trade shows, association meetings and other events in order to meet and build relationships with supplier diversity professionals, GME organizations and your fellow certified businesses. The good news is that the supplier diversity community offers abundant opportunities for business owner Davids to meet corporate Goliaths. Meet-and-greet opportunities are part of the industry's standard practice.

A look at my calendar shows that I practice what I preach. As I write this chapter, I am also networking at an IBM Regional Supplier Diversity Town Meeting. In just the first session this morning I have reconnected with Karen Ritter, WBENC's corporate representative from Goldman Sachs. Karen and I are working on the development of an internationally-focused project and have had trouble connecting on the phone. This unscheduled opportunity allowed us to catch up and plan future strategies.

Thus far today I also talked with a minority woman business owner we have been trying to convince to become WBENC-certified (she informed me her application is in process), met the Director of the newly formed Gay and Lesbian Chamber of Commerce, talked with several IBM executives and sat through a presentation on access to capital for suppliers. Believe it or not, it is only 9:00 a.m.! Three of WBENC's regional affiliates have staff here and a dozen of our certified WBEs are also here. It is clear to me that I am not "away from my business," merely out of the office. My business is wherever I am. Yours should be, too.

Throughout this chapter, keep in mind that, just like your marketing activities, your networking tactics must be strategic and consistent to be effective. Association dues, trade show fees and high-tech database management systems can become expensive and time consuming, so educate yourself about all of the available opportunities, and then pick and choose what will work for your particular business and industry segment. All GMEs—and all GME networking practices—need not be the same.

Finally, remember to relax and have a bit of fun while you are networking. Making genuine connections with other businesspeople in the GME community can be one of the most rewarding and enjoyable aspects of business ownership. Most of these professionals are passionate about their work and derive enormous satisfaction from helping to maximize each other's success.

Getting to Know You: Associations and Networking Organizations

One of the first steps to building a good network is to join organizations that offer opportunities to meet and connect with other businesspeople with whom you share an industry, community or other affinity. Hundreds of thousands of organizations exist, some as small as five or six people, others as large as major corporations. Depending on your interests, business needs and time availability, many associations and networking groups are likely to appeal to you.

Given all of these options, how do you decide which memberships are worthwhile? There is no correct number of association memberships to have, so you will have to decide what makes sense for you. Some business owners only belong to one or two associations and become extremely active, while others find value in receiving the publications and member benefits of several additional organizations.

Here are some suggestions for vetting which associations and networking groups are worth the membership dues. Keep these tips in mind as you read through the organizations described on the next several pages:

- Ask friends and colleagues in your industry what associations they belong to and/or recommend. If it seems like "everyone" belongs, then you should too.
- As you begin to develop relationships with corporate supplier diversity professionals, seek their guidance. Many corporations recognize the competitive advantage association membership can provide to their suppliers and they will recommend certain memberships over others. Sometimes companies will even foot the bill. Merrill Lynch recently sponsored the membership of 12 WBE suppliers to join the prestigious Women Presidents' Organization. (For more

information about WPO, refer to the section on "Mastermind Groups," below.)

- Visit the website of each association (and each association's local chapter, if applicable) you are considering. Check closely for information about:
  - Membership Dues – Be on the lookout for lower prices if you join for multiple years at one time, or if you join during a special "membership drive."
  - Membership Benefits – Often the benefits available to association members, such as free subscriptions to industry publications or discounts on event attendance, justify the annual membership dues.
  - Publications – Does the association offer members a magazine, newsletter or e-newsletter? As discussed in the previous chapter on marketing, industry publications are one of the best ways to educate yourself about your potential customers and competitors and to promote yourself as a contributor or interview subject. Pay special attention to the corporations that advertise in these publications.
  - Events and Workshops – How often does the association host conferences, networking events or educational workshops in your area? Does the organization host tele-classes or web seminars? Will membership guarantee you will receive invitations to these events? Are there separate fees to attend these events and can non-members attend at a higher price?
  - Membership Directory or Database – If you join this association, will you receive a directory of members, and will you be able to promote yourself to your fellow members? Is the directory in print or electronic? The latter is more likely to be kept current.
  - Special Interest Groups – If the association is particularly large, does it offer smaller affinity groups that meet

your particular needs? For instance, do they offer a women's group, a marketers' group, a finance group, etc.? Often these special interest groups will have their own area on the association's website, their own meetings and their own publications. The National Association of Women in Construction, for example, has separate activities and opportunities for entrepreneurial members.

- ○ Board of Directors – Who sits on the association's board? These "VIPs" will offer insight into the caliber of the association.

- Take a test drive. While most associations do not offer trial memberships, it is worthwhile to call and request free attendance at an event or a free copy of the association's most recent communication so you can check them out before committing. If this is not possible and you are uncertain about joining a particular association, do try to attend at least one association-sponsored event before committing to any high-cost membership dues.

Keeping the above issues in mind, here is a comprehensive guide to the wide variety of organizations that exist and the opportunities each offers to GMEs interested in selling to large corporations.

Industry Associations

If you have not already, I highly recommend that you join the most prominent trade association in your industry. From the National Electrical Manufacturers Association to the Women's Food Forum to the International Franchise Association to the Independent Computer Consultants Association to the American Translators Association, I can virtually guarantee that a trade group exists, no matter what your field. (For a comprehensive list of over 6,500 associations, visit the "Gateway to Associations" on the website of the American Society of Association Executives at *www.asaenet.org.*)

Some industry associations offer the option to join a local chapter, while others provide their services from a single national headquarters. Larger industries often have a few competing associations serving their community. It is perfectly fine (though not always necessary) to join all associations in your industry, depending on your needs.

The main advantages of industry association membership include highly specialized publications and educational opportunities, mentoring programs to learn from more advanced people in your field (or to give back to those just starting out) and political lobbying on behalf of your group's interests.

Most industry associations collect data on pricing policies, industry-specific government regulations, salaries and trends that can be enormously helpful. Your membership dues may be repaid many times over by access to this information.

Organizations for Certified Businesses

Joining an organization in this category should not require any thought—it is 100 percent essential to take advantage of this networking gold mine. As advised earlier, upon receiving your certification you should make contact with the regional or local affiliate that processed your certification. Simply call and introduce yourself and ask for a calendar of upcoming events in your area. Upon approval of your certification, most will automatically add you to their e-mail notification system that disseminates interesting business information and local and national event announcements, but a personal call is still important. Connection to these groups will ensure that you have access to expert advice and the most current resources available regarding supplier diversity in your region.

Note: If you do not personally review the e-mail that comes in to your company, make certain that you are notified of these important business opportunities. At a minimum, you should make certain that WBENC's monthly *President's Report* and our "RFP" blast e-mail system—*WEBuy@wbenc.org*—go directly to you to insure that you do not miss valuable opportunities. If you do not currently receive this information, send a request to *B2B@wbenc.org* and ask that your e-mail address be added to the list.

WBENC and the NMSDC work with local affiliates that provide a variety of networking opportunities to businesses holding certifications. As you will recall from previous chapters, WBENC's affiliates include regional Women's Business Organization Partners (WBOPs) and the NMSDC has regional councils.

Regional WBOPs, some of which charge separate membership dues or event fees (above and beyond the certification fee that they collect to process your application and site visit), provide highly specialized advice and networking opportunities for certified women's business enterprises. Note that the WBOPs that charge a membership fee return that part of the fee (but not the non-refundable processing fee) if you are denied certification.

Each of these affiliates (as listed in Appendix B), has a Women's Enterprise Leadership Forum made up of WBEs who share the desire to expand their contracting opportunities with America's corporations. If you are a WBENC-certified WBE, I highly recommend that you join a local Forum. Two members of each local Forum are nominated to represent local interests on WBENC's National Forum—pretty powerful! WBENC corporate members can also nominate WBEs with whom they are currently doing business for national Forum membership. National Forum meetings and local Forum events are high-level networking opportunities where connections are made that lead to business opportunities. Nine national Forum members serve on the WBENC Board of Directors for three-year terms. Every WBENC-certified business is eligible for this exclusive access, so do not be shy about raising your hand for a Forum opportunity.

As you can see, the most obvious benefit of certification-related organizations is the targeted nature of their mission. Leaders of these groups know that their business owner members want to network with corporate purchasing executives, so they regularly provide such opportunities. For instance, New York's Women Presidents' Educational Organization, run by Marsha Firestone, Ph.D., sponsors an annual "Breakthrough Breakfast" at which certified WBEs interact with a few dozen corporate purchasing officers. Throughout the year, WBENC affiliates conduct corporate/WBE networking events that range from educational panels and seminars to multi-day business fairs and conferences. WBENC's *President's Report*, referenced previously, carries up-to-date information on events across the country all year, and you can access a WBENC calendar of events at *www.wbenc.org*. Check back at the website on a regular basis to stay current on new opportunities for world-class networking events.

WBENC's own national conference, **Women in Business: Sharing the Vision**, is held annually at the end of June. The four-day event, chock-full of formal and informal networking opportunities, is a business networker's paradise. The first day features the annual national Women's Enterprise Leadership Forum meeting, a new event in 2006 and one that we hope will be repeated. Among the attendees will be members of The Zenith Group, WBENC's program for woman-owned companies whose annual revenues exceed $50 million. Networking opportunities include the chance to get to know these women CEOs, whose own purchasing programs provide Second Tier spend for their top corporate customers.

The conference also offers workshops, plenary sessions and receptions that impart valuable information while simultaneously providing the opportunity to meet and greet corporate representatives. Wednesday of conference week is dedicated to the business fair, where more than 400 exhibitors set up booths and provide opportunities throughout the day for business interaction. Even the breakfasts, lunches and evening events provide forums for WBEs and corporate purchasing and supplier diversity executives to meet and exchange information. On Thursday, prescheduled one-on-one "MatchMaker Meetings" (see Chapter Five for more information on these opportunities) start things off, and workshops provide cutting-edge information on supply chain trends and practices.

Other large-scale WBE events include conferences hosted by the Women's Business Development Center in Chicago every September (*www.wbdc.org*); Women's Business Enterprise Alliance in Houston (*www.wbea-texas.org*); the Women's Business Council Southwest each May (*www.wbcsouthwest.org*); and the Michigan Women's Business Council in October (734-677-1400).

The broad network of regional councils associated with the NMSDC also conduct regional business fairs. The NMSDC's national conference is usually held the last week of October and attracts thousands of business owners and purchasing officials to a four-day event. The NMSDC national website (*www.nmsdcus.org*) also provides a state-by-state listing of local MBE trade fairs and events.

Spotlight: "Our Best Marketing Strategy"

WBE Marsha Rose Davidson, President of Telecopy, Inc. says that the best marketing strategy for her business has been becoming actively involved with her local WBENC affiliate, the Women's Business Council Southwest (WBCS):

"After I was certified, I was advised by the two corporate members who performed my site visit to get involved with the council in order to get the maximum benefits from my certification. Those were words of gold.

"My first two years, I was co-chair of 'Done Deals™' committee. Then I helped form our 'Welcoming Committee' and served as co-chair of that committee for two years. I am currently on the Executive Board of Directors, co-chair of our membership input services committee, WBE Ambassador for the council and one of the council's WBENC forum representatives. Each of our committees is chaired by a WBE and a corporate member, so my committee work has enabled me to develop relationships that, in turn, have helped me to get business from corporations.

"I have also been able to meet and develop relationships with many WBEs through my involvement with the council. Fellow certified businesses have assisted me by providing contacts in many of the corporations that I could not get on my own.

"I cannot emphasize enough how important it is for WBEs to become involved with their local councils. Not only have I developed wonderful relationships, but I have also gained the trust of many of the corporations because they have seen me throughout the last five years. Get active—the rewards are invaluable!"

Chambers of Commerce

Chambers of Commerce provide another easy way to become involved in your local community of entrepreneurs. Chambers include a sampling of businesses of all shapes and sizes in your town or city. Membership dues generally range from a few hundred to a few thousand dollars based on the size of your business. While you may or may not come across corporate purchasers at meetings of your local chamber, you will connect with contacts who can refer you in the right direction, as well as potential vendors, partners, advisers and friends.

Additionally, local Chambers host business fairs, workshops, conferences and other events that can be beneficial in and of themselves, or can serve as a nice "training ground" for the bigger corporate events or trade shows you will attend later. In many big cities, large corporations are active members of the local chamber of commerce.

On the national level, the U.S. Chamber of Commerce is the world's largest business federation, representing over three million American businesses including women and minority business owners. The Chamber's diversity outreach initiative promotes the Chamber's pro-business policy agenda, cutting-edge information and resources, and a vast array of educational and networking programs that support diverse audiences nation-wide. The U.S. Chamber's executive director for diversity outreach, Rita Perlman, recommends Chamber membership to GMEs:

> "The U.S. Chamber addresses the needs of women and minority business leaders through our global feder-ation of state, local and international chambers. The Chamber works to advance issues of importance to busi-nesses, including healthcare, tax reform and workforce strategies for businesses, chambers of commerce and communities to hire, train, retain and advance skilled workers in the 21st Century. Through the U.S. Chamber's Small Business Center at *www.uschamber.com/sb*, members can access unparalleled tools and resources that can help them grow and expand their businesses, as well as learn how to become advocates for business."

For more information about Chamber membership, specific events and resources, visit *www.uschamber.com*.

Large ethnic Chambers, such as the U.S. Hispanic Chamber of Commerce (*www.ushcc.com*) and the National Black Chamber of Commerce (*www.nationalbcc.org*) provide similar opportunities both regionally and nationally. Susan Au Allen, president and CEO of the U.S. Pan Asian American Chamber of Commerce (*www.uspaacc.com*), invites Asian American business owners to learn more about this organization:

> "Formed in 1984, the U.S. Pan Asian American Chamber of Commerce is a vital voice for the Pan Asian American business community. We advocate for equal procurement opportunities for Asian Americans before major corporations, government agencies and the United States Congress.   By opening the doors of contract, professional and educational opportunities to those who seek them, we help to nurture, develop and grow small businesses into medium-size and then large businesses."

Women and Minority Associations

As more and more women and minorities have taken on leadership roles in business, organizations have formed to provide unique networking and educational opportunities within these communities. Some of the larger professional women's groups in this category include the National Association of Women Business Owners (*www.nawbo.org*), American Business Women's Association (*www.abwa.org*), Business & Professional Women USA (*www.bpwusa.org*) and the National Association for Female Executives (*www.nafe.com*). Large national minority associations, in addition to the chambers listed above, include the Latin Business Association (*www.lbausa.com*), the National Minority Business Council (*www.nmbc.org*) and the National Indian Business Association (*www.nibanetwork.org*).

In addition to these large organizations, which provide networking opportunities among businesses of a wide variety of sizes, industries and geographic locations, many smaller women's and minority groups exist within industries. Examples include the National Society of Black Engineers (*www.nsbe.org*), National Association of Minority Contractors (*www.namcline.org*), Women in Technology International (*www.witi.com*) and the National Association of Women in Construction (*www.nawic.org*).

Like industry associations, many women's and minority organizations provide member benefits, conferences and events, publications, leadership opportunities, mentoring programs and attention to political issues affecting their members. And, with any organization, there are great opportunities to make new friends. WBE Mary Kay Hamm, president of Linden International, encourages fellow WBEs to value their women's business network. "It is extremely rich, because it gives you the power of support. I have stayed alive in recessions because of the girlfriends I met through WBENC!"

"Mastermind" Groups

Mastermind groups consist of a small number of like-minded business people who meet on a regular basis to share goals and support one another in business success. You can find groups that are industry-specific or include representatives of diverse businesses. Many certified business owners find it helpful to form or join a mastermind group of other certified GMEs. The sharing of resources, contacts and advice in an intimate setting can be invaluable.

The Women Presidents' Organization, with 55 chapters in 41 cities in the United States and Canada, is among the more formal mastermind organizations. The WPO limits participation in each of its peer mentoring groups to 20 entrepreneurs led by a professional facilitator. Only businesses that generate at least $2 million in gross annual sales (or $1 million for service-based businesses) are eligible to participate. Additionally, WPO offers a Platinum Group, which brings together WPO members with revenues of $10 million and above, to address their specific needs.

In 2005, WBENC and the WPO joined forces to launch an additional mastermind program for fast growth woman-owned firms, called the Zenith Group. This new program works to maximize the effectiveness and competitiveness of WBE firms with revenues in excess of $50 million. The Zenith Group brings together highly motivated, highly successful, certified entrepreneurial women in a dynamic forum where they can harness the momentum of their successes and aim for bigger profits and bigger dreams. Zenith Group members can attend power meetings enabling them to meet privately with decision makers at leading corporations seeking their products or services. Zenith Group also gives its members an intensive immersion in management topics for their size of business, from human resources and employee benefits to corporate purchasing and procurement, and the opportunity to create strategic alliances among the Zenith Group members themselves. For more information about the WPO or the Zenith Group, visit *www.womenpresidentsorg.com*.

If you cannot find an existing mastermind group that suits your needs, go ahead and start your own. Associations and certification listservs are a great place to recruit potential members.

Making the Most of Your Memberships

Associations exist to serve the needs of members like you, so let them do their job! If you have employees, use your staff strategically—especially your sales team—and assign each to specific associations. Their networking efforts will expand the opportunities for your firm.

Here are several suggestions on how to maximize your organization memberships to help grow your business and attract corporate contracts:

- Say hello. Introduce yourself to the leaders of associations to which you belong, on both the national and local levels. Remember, successful networking means that people must know who you are and what you do. Call and say hello, or introduce yourself at an association event. Speaking as the president of a large organization, I can tell you that I am thrilled to meet WBENC-certified WBEs at events around the country. Do not be shy!

- List yourself and your business in member directories. This is another obvious strategy. As with supplier diversity databases, make sure that your association member listings remain current and fully describe the capabilities of your business. You never know where a potential customer will find you. And be certain to keep electronic databases up-to-date with correct contact information including any changes to your e-mail address.

- Read the member database. Scour the listings of members to find people in the companies or industries you are targeting as customers. I do not recommend cold calling every potential lead in your association, but you may consider a targeted mailing to these people or asking an association leader to make a personal introduction. (Do not waste money on mailings unless they are professional in appearance and you have a good plan for following up.) This is also a good place to find vendors and strategic partners to help you grow your business.

- Join online listservs. Listservs are online discussion groups. In a listserv, association members or other interest groups may "subscribe" to a given discussion, and other subscribers' contributions to the discussion are distributed to the subscriber base via e-mail. The experience is similar to a newsgroup or forum, except that the messages are transmitted by e-mail and are only available to individuals on the particular list. Listservs are great for discussing current events in your industry, asking for advice and finding support from your peers. And, if you are not in the mood to participate one day, all you need to do is click "delete."

As previously mentioned, all WBENC-certified WBEs and corporate members can take advantage of both *WBENC-Discuss@wbenc.org*, which provides information on meetings and events as well as current issues of importance to business owners, and *WEBuy@wbenc.org*, where RFPs, "sources sought" and matchmaking opportunities are posted. Be sure to make certain, as I stated above, that whomever you delegate the e-mail assignment to understands the value to your company of these opportunities and forwards the e-mail accordingly to the appropriate contact within your company.

- Take on an active leadership role. Raise your hand for committees, board positions and other responsibilities (such as WBENC forums mentioned above) that will teach you new skills, introduce you to key people in your association and provide you with opportunities to build your reputation in the organization. Prove yourself to be a visible, responsible leader.
- Contribute to association publications. As discussed, most large associations have multiple online and print publications. Send in your news and press releases for member news areas. Offer to write by-lined articles on topics of interest to association members. Call the editor of each publication and volunteer yourself as an "expert" resource on topics related to your business.
- Speak. Connect with the programming director of any organization of which you are a member and find out the procedure for speaking at an event. Many associations are pleased to present seminars and workshops featuring the expertise of their own members.
- Apply for awards. Member of the Year, Mentor of the Year,

Volunteer of the Year—most associations honor several members annually. Local and national certification organizations offer many impressive award opportunities as well. Winning an award is great publicity and catapults you to visibility and status in your organization, in your community and in your industry. Even the act of applying demonstrates your motivation to association leaders and award evaluation committees. When you win, do not forget to widely distribute a press release concerning the award or honor, particularly to corporations you are pitching. An added bonus is that accepting the award generally gives you a visible networking opportunity at the award event or ceremony.

- Be charitable. Donate one of your products (or provide a gift certificate if your business does not produce an appropriate item) to an association-sponsored auction. This raises your profile and shows that you are willing to give back to your organization and its members.

- Be a mentor and help other people to meet their goals. I have a cousin who just founded his own law firm. An expert on DNA defenses, Robbie, at the request of a friend, spent several meetings with a 54-year-old retired and successful entrepreneur who wanted to go back to school to become an attorney so that he too could, pro bono, provide DNA defenses to unjustly incarcerated individuals. As an after-thought at the conclusion of their second lunch, Robbie asked if he could get some advice on how to build a successful business—his law firm. While he was an experienced attorney, "rain making" was new to him. His guest told him to take out a pencil and proceeded to provide a list of ten successful friends—all business owners. Furthermore, he told Robbie to tell these people that he said Robbie was a "first rate" attorney who should be considered to handle their business' legal needs. Needless to say, the few hours Robbie spent with this gentleman paid off in spades for his new law firm. A friendship was born as well.

- Buy advertising. If you have the marketing budget and your association includes some of your corporate prospects as members, consider buying classified or full-page advertising in an important industry publication.

- Show up, again and again. All of the above strategies for maximizing your association memberships will be infinitely more effective the more you show your face at association events and meet your fellow members.

Membership Has Its Privileges

Still need more reasons to join an association or networking group? Two association leaders share their perspective: "Membership means different things to different people, but entails some sort of emotional commitment, as well as a financial commitment.

"On a national level, the primary value of association membership is through numbers—being able to say that you have joined a group of hundreds or thousands to convene around an issue that you think is vital to your community, profession, business or belief system. For instance, it is powerful to announce that 10,000 women entrepreneurs believe that Congress should consider certain legislation and programs, and it is useful to present the aggregate amount of people they employ, funds they channel into the economy, and their overall contribution to our country's economic growth.

"On a local level, membership allows access to networking events and educational programs, which are very important in order to build business contacts and gain access to experts that can assist with financing, marketing and strategic development."

- Erin Fuller, executive director
National Association of Women Business Owners (NAWBO)

"When you are part of an organization that espouses the principles (business or otherwise) that you believe in, then you have the opportunity to make your voice heard. Although there are many solo crusaders throughout history who have fought valiantly for a cause they believe in, most of the successful ones have inspired, motivated and engaged others to join with them. An impassioned group, working together, can change the course of history. The power of many voices joined together as one voice is undeniable."
- Barbara Kasoff, co-founder and president
Women Impacting Public Policy (WIPP)

Attending Networking Events

Meetings, conferences, workshops and social outings are where the very best connections are established and nurtured. Whether attending an event hosted by an association to which you belong or that of another organization, follow these strategies for getting the most out of your attendance:

- Do your homework. Learn as much as you can about the event, the sponsoring organization, the speakers and the attendees before you attend. With a simple "Google" Internet search on the name of the keynote speaker, you may learn that he or she sits on the board of your top corporate prospect.

- Arrive early. The earlier you arrive, the more chances you will have to chat with the organizers of the event and the most eager attendees. You will also have the time to get a good seat, read any provided materials and feel comfortable.

- Mention your membership. Include mention of your certification and/or your association affiliation when you introduce yourself to new people. "My name is Janet Smith and I own a certified Woman Business Enterprise in the garment manufacturing industry."

- Bring materials. In addition to the essential stack of business cards (when in doubt, bring more than you think you will need—there is no excuse for running out of cards and writing on the back of a napkin), go ahead and bring brochures, product samples or marketing materials. They may stay in your tote bag or briefcase, but you will be happy to have these materials if you meet a strong prospect. Make sure your certification clearly appears on all materials. This will be an instant signal to any supplier diversity attendees you meet.

- Aside from formal events, I never travel without a stack of brochures in my carry-on luggage. You never know who will be in the next seat on the plane. Furthermore, if your certification body provides pins or other "markers," you should wear them proudly on your lapel as yet another indicator of your status. For example, WBENC members, both WBEs and corporations that support our annual fundraiser, the Salute to Women's Business Enterprises, receive a complimentary pin commemorating the event.

- Do not act desperate to make contacts. Recognize that others are evaluating you, so be professional, courteous and keep a positive attitude at all times.

- Do not go it alone. If you are shy, bring a networking buddy—a fellow businessperson who is not there to keep you company near the food table, but rather to encourage you to talk to new people. Sometimes a little extra push is all you need.

- Go outside your comfort zone. Even if you are not shy, the danger of being too active in a networking organization is that you will want to spend events chatting with your friends.

While it is important to keep up existing contacts (and by all means spend some time with your pals and existing customers), make a concerted effort to meet new people at every event you attend.

- Be name-tag savvy. When you can, list both your name and your business on your name tag. Help people connect you and your face with your company. You may even consider purchasing your own name tag to ensure that your name and company name are in a large enough type font to be clearly read. This also guarantees correct spelling and avoids inappropriate nicknames and other errors.

- Meet the speakers. Go right up and introduce yourself to the event's speakers or panelists. They are there not only to speak but also to network, so do not be shy. If you do feel intimidated, this situation comes with the perfect ice breaker. "I am really looking forward to your talk," works every time. If the speaker has written a book or article, read it in advance so that you can say, "I read your article in *MBE Magazine* and would like to ask..."

- Take notes. Besides writing down interesting information provided in the formal program, take note of the names of people you have met and any follow-up required. You can do this on a pad or PDA, or it is always smart to make notes on the back of people's business cards so you remember who is who.

- Follow up. Immediately follow up with all important contacts made at a networking function. Within a week (or preferably a day or two), send a brief e-mail, make a phone call or send a card and keep the relationship going. This is truly what defines smart networkers. Particularly with potential customers, show that you are a person who follows up and keeps his or her word. Keep your promises of "We must get together!" and you will end up ahead of the pack.

Spotlight: "Schlepping and Schmoozing"

How has WBE Heidi Berenson of Berenson Communications, Inc, landed business with the likes of Capital One, IBM, Freddie Mac and Pfizer? She calls her success strategy "Schlepping and Schmoozing." Heidi says, "Quite simply, I position myself in front of key executives as much as possible—establishing a rapport—since people buy based on how they feel rather than on what they see or hear. To that end, I attend as many WBENC and WPEO events as possible and also volunteer to lead workshops that showcase my communication coaching talents. This approach plants the seeds, and sharing anecdotes from training my Fortune 500 clients fertilizes growth."

Heidi offers this three-step strategy for networking and sales success:

- Establish a relationship with key executives, whether supplier diversity or other contacts.
- Provide them with impressive examples of high-level clients to establish your track record of success.
- Demonstrate your capabilities so that just like a sample in a bakery, they get a taste of your talent.

Consider adding the "Schlepping and Schmoozing" concept to your networking plan of action.

Networking Nirvana: Supplier Diversity Trade Shows & Buyers' Marts

Early in my career, when I was a manufacturers' representative covering a six-state New England territory, I attended my industry's national annual trade show at the Waldorf-Astoria Hotel in New York City. It was great—all of my customers and potential customers from throughout my territory and around the country were gathered in one place. I knew it was my big chance and I took full advantage. It was a time and money saver for me to be able to meet with clients from northern Maine and southwestern Rhode Island all in the same place with no driving and not having to lug sample cases in and out of the trunk of my car. To me, trade shows and business fairs are like speed-dating parties: a huge number of prospects in one place—which, to be honest, can be a potential jackpot or a scary and overwhelming circus! This section will put business fairs and trade shows into perspective.

For certified businesses, numerous trade shows exist at the local and national level. If you wanted, you could probably attend a trade show or business expo every week! I recommend obtaining calendars of supplier diversity business fairs (and other events) from many sources so you have a comprehensive list to review if you are considering participation:

- WBENC's website (*www.wbenc.org*) shares information on its national events, including online registration for attendees, sponsors and exhibitors. You can also connect to the websites of each of our regional affiliates.
- NMSDC's website has a state-by-state trade show calendar (*www.nmsdcus.org*)
- Check corporate supplier diversity websites of companies such as Microsoft and Office Depot (Office Depot even hosts its own event, the annual Success Strategies for Businesswomen Conference)
- Supplier diversity industry publications such as *MBE (Minority Business Entrepreneur) Magazine, Minority Business Insider, WE,* or *Enterprising Women.*
- TradeNet (*www.tradenet.gov*), the U.S. government's website trade show calendar, provided by the Department of Commerce
- If you are a WBENC member, the monthly *President's Report*

provides information on national and regional events.
- E-zines available from websites such as *www.SBTV.com*, *www.WomensCalendar.org* and *www.WE-Inc.org* provide calendars

Yes, trade shows offer an amazing opportunity to meet corporate buyers face-to-face, but, just like speed-dating parties, they are not for everyone at all times. You may want to visit trade shows as an attendee only—to network and make face-to-face connections, or you may make exhibiting with a trade show booth a large component of your marketing plan. Here are the key issues to consider when making the decision on how to participate:

- **Do you have the budget to buy a booth, travel to the event and cover accommodation expenses?** Booths can cost from several hundred to several thousand dollars, depending on the size and caliber of the event and the booth's design. Remember, this is not a retail show, so you will not be selling your products at your booth, only displaying enough information to entice corporate buyers to learn more about you.
- **Will your prospects be attending?** Business fairs list their corporate sponsors, exhibitors and speakers on their websites, often months in advance, so you should be able to gather this information. Do not invest in a booth if your potential buyers are not attending. However, you may want to attend as a non-exhibitor to check out other GMEs or make other networking contacts.
- **Will you have help staffing your booth?** Particularly for multi-day business fairs, you will want an employee or other informed person to help staff your booth if you plan to walk around the event or attend seminars and meals. Audrey Goins Brichi, manager of supplier diversity and small business programs at Chevron, says that GMEs really stand out

at a trade show when they have "the right people in the booth with the right answers for our buyers." Most exhibitor fees will include attendance for more than one representative of your company so the additional cost is small compared to the opportunity offered.

- **Do you have a professional-looking booth?** Your professional image is extremely important at a trade show. As with your marketing materials, your trade show display (whether a full booth or a table-top) must show that you are capable of "playing in the big leagues." If you cannot do it right, do not do it. You will also want to invest in a token "give-away" that is branded with your corporate name, and a phone number or website address. Once you have invested in your booth, you will be able to amortize its cost across many events. Some businesses display their booths in the lobby area of their companies, providing an attractive alternative use.

When you do make the decision to exhibit at a supplier diversity trade show, here are tips from experienced GMEs on how to work a trade show like a pro:

- Find out who you want to see – Again, research all exhibitors, sponsors, speakers and other attendees. Find out which competitors, corporate buyers, association leaders, VIPs and other good contacts will be attending. Know who you want to target, where their booths or workshops are located and how you plan to approach them. This may mean crisscrossing the trade show floor but it will insure that you have an opportunity to see your target firms. Lynn Boccio, vice president, Strategic Business and Diversity Relations of Avis Rent A Car and Budget Rent A Car, is impressed when business fair attendees show that they have researched her company before approaching the booth. "Having background about our company demonstrates that they have done their homework and have targeted our firm as one of interest—and not just another booth to drop a business card," she says.

- Consider volunteering your time or expertise – Contact the organizers to offer your products or services in exchange for an ad in the event program or other valuable exposure. Kerry Hammer, of the WBENC-certified Hammer Press, donated her printing services to the annual WBENC conference and business fair in 2003. In return, she was featured as an event sponsor and had a four-color ad in the program book, all of which attracted the attention of some major buyers. Conference co-sponsor Altria followed up by researching her firm and selecting Hammer Press to print its supplier diversity brochure. She has also printed supplier diversity brochures for Pfizer, HBO and Time Warner.

- Organize an event within the event – Another Kerry Hammer gem: Knowing many of her existing clients and prospect customers would be attending the Women in Business: Sharing the Vision business fair and conference in New York City for which she bartered for a sponsorship, Kerry invited her contacts at these companies to join her for a taping of the Late Show with David Letterman. This unique (and fun!) hospitality impressed her VIPs and gave her hours of additional one-on-one contact.

- Participate in silent auctions and raffles – It can be worth the investment to bid on some of the business-related offerings at a trade show's raffle. Many silent auctions nowadays feature the prize of "lunch with a CEO or CPO (chief purchasing officer)." This unique opportunity has proven more than worth the cost for such certified WBEs as Nancy Michaels, whose $1,050 bid for lunch with former Office Depot CEO Bruce Nelson led to one of the largest contracts of her lifetime. Donna Cole of Cole Chemical in Houston took this concept one step further: She bid $6,000 for lunch with the Chief Purchasing Officer of Shell. When their lunch date arrived, Donna, who has a passion for cooking, used herbs from her garden and made a spectacular Asian fusion lunch for the CPO and his managers. The Shell team toured Cole's headquarters and marveled at the wall murals depicting Asian, African and Native American women in cultural dress going about their daily lives. The purchasing officer not only appreciated the experience, but also learned an enormous amount about Cole Chemical. At the time, Cole was losing opportunities due to bundling and global contracts, and the visit helped Donna begin a dialogue to carve out strategic pieces of business for her company. Nancy Williams of ASAP Staffing in Atlanta takes another creative and successful approach when she wins an auction, inviting the executive to a round of golf at an exclusive club.

- Network with other suppliers – Do not focus all of your attention on potential customers. Take time to meet business owners who supply your current customers and may be potential strategic partners. Trade shows can also be a great place to meet potential mastermind group members or to form barter relationships.

- Attend workshops and meals – It does not all happen on the trade show floor! Do not spend *all* of your time at your booth. Some of the best connections are made in other settings, particularly during informal moments like breaks, unscheduled evenings, receptions and continental break-fasts where seating is not assigned. Tempted to shop the local boutiques? Invite a prospect to join you for an outing to a special or favorite store.

- Collect business cards at your booth for a raffle – Ideally you should hold a raffle for one of your products. This is a great way to attract visitors to your booth and collect names for your mailing list at the same time. The winner, of course, gets to sample your product for free—and will feel good about it!

- Bring more than enough marketing materials – Never run out. The trade show website will give you a basic idea of the number of event attendees you can expect. Plus, little gimmicks like chocolates or, better yet, clever trinkets branded with your company name, are great for drawing people into your booth. A tip on trinkets—give something that will really be used—and used often—by your prospects, such as pens, note pads or magnets. Yoyos and such are cute, but most people throw them in the trash after a spin or two or give them to a child. In 2005, WBENC asked WBE firm Java Technologies to produce a cell phone "charm" with the WBENC logo for everyone who stopped by the WBENC booth. Corporations also use giveaways to enhance their brand. At the 2005 NMSDC conference in Dallas, Texas, Home Depot's bright orange bags were a huge hit. Large enough and strong enough (and purchased by Home Depot from a WBE firm) to hold lots of materials and giveaways, the bags could be spotted throughout the conference and even at the airport as attendees were departing.

- Follow up, Follow up, Follow up – Diane McClelland, co-founder and president of Astra Women's Business Alliance, advises GMEs always to follow up in a timely manner after meeting at an event. This shows that you are serious about making a real connection. Trade shows can be exhausting, so by all means take a day or two to recover. But then, your first order of business is to pursue every lead made at a trade show. Make your investment worthwhile by thanking all guests at your booth, saying "nice to meet you" to all new contacts and answering any questions posed to you by booth visitors.

- Do not sit down and do not stand behind a table. I know it is tiring, but plan ahead and wear comfortable shoes. At the end of the WBENC business fair I sometimes feel that I cannot stand up for one minute longer. Tables create barriers between you and your prospects and you project more energy standing than seated.

- If you have your booth number ahead of time, print cards that you can distribute at networking events that direct people to your booth.
- Write to your prospects and current clients inviting them to drop by.

Spotlight: Deals done on the spot at trade shows!

Sorry to disappoint, but this almost never happens. Do not go to a trade show expecting a deal to be done on the spot. "Success" should be defined as getting a contact to follow up with. If you attend a trade show thinking you are going to get That One Big Contract to save your company from bankruptcy, you may as well try to win the money in Vegas. While trade shows can reap huge rewards for your company in the long run, keep your short-term expectations in check.

Host Your Own Networking Events

Tired of traveling to events? Bring the networking to you. Consider celebrating a new product launch or business anniversary with a gathering of your contacts. If you have an impressive office or warehouse, hold the event in your space and offer tours to educate your guests about your business capabilities. Even if some invitees do not attend, they will learn of your success through your invitations.

Michelle Boggs of McKinley Marketing Partners incorporates her own events throughout the year for clients and prospects. A member of WBENC's Board of Directors and National Forum, she invited all forum and board members to a reception at her firm's distinctive office in Old Town Alexandria in conjunction with a quarterly meeting. Her impressive office space as well as her generosity is a good showcase for her company. The event was a big success and gave each of the attendees a more personal connection to Michelle and her business.

Networking Mistakes to Avoid

There are many different ways to network well. But always be sure your networking is courteous and positive. Here are some networking mistakes that can sink your efforts:

- Bruce Perkins of Merrill Lynch advises GMEs never to say you are too busy to take advantage of opportunities offered by a corporation. For instance, Merrill provides education sponsorships at Dartmouth's Tuck School of Business, Northwestern's Kellogg School, and the University of Wisconsin/Madison, but some GMEs have declined such an opportunity, claiming that they are too busy. This is a quick way to turn off a supplier diversity supporter. Of course, you must concentrate on paying bills, but be sure to take advantage of maximum opportunities for growth, networking and increasing core competencies. Do not refuse free help!
- Craig Adams, chief supply officer at Exelon, warns against the dangers of impatient networking. "Do not overpressure," he says. "That does not work well. I get a lot of pressure all the time at work! You should be deliberate, but not overbearing when interacting with a supplier diversity professional. The best approach is to tell me that you want to add value: 'Here is where I am now and I would like to understand what is next from your perspective.'" According to Craig, networking in the supplier diversity community—and any business environment for that matter—calls for "a mix of patience and tenacity." Be sure your mix is balanced before you pick up that phone to follow up for the fourteenth time!

Networking Follow-up

No matter which associations you join and which events you choose to attend or host, networking is a marathon, not a sprint. Follow-up and regular contact (but not too much) are essential to maintaining the contacts you work so hard to cultivate. It takes time to get to the finish line.

You will no doubt develop your own style of follow-up and communication depending on your business size, industry, prospect list and personality. Here are some tips—again, for you to pick and choose for yourself—on maintaining your connections:

- Pick up a pen – While we all love the ease and immediacy of e-mail, sometimes a handwritten note can do wonders for a business relationship. A "thank you," "nice to meet you," "thought this article would interest you" or other communication can brighten someone's day and show that you are a business owner willing to take a little extra time for your clients and friends.

- Build a strong database – Take the time to research and invest in the best database or contact management system you can afford. Popular choices include ACT, Microsoft Outlook and FileMaker Pro. I gave up my Rolodex of business cards years ago to gain the flexibility of Microsoft Outlook. I even have it synced to my Sprint Treo phone that includes e-mail, addresses and telephone numbers all in one place. It is the most valuable tool I have found in the past ten years to help me communicate while I am on the road. Computerized databases are also essential these days for easy sorting, creating mailing labels and keeping track of phone call and meeting notes. Immediately update your database when you receive news of an address change so your list is always 100 percent current. As soon as I return from a business fair or conference, I have all my new contacts added to my database.

- Maintain regular contact – It is important to reach out to your entire database at least once a year to stay on everyone's radar screen. Many people choose the December holiday season to send a mailing. Another option is to celebrate your business' anniversary each year with a card and perhaps a small gift. We at WBENC picked up a good tip at a "Perfecting Your Pitch" workshop conducted by WBE Nancy Michaels, president of Impression Impact, at a WBENC MatchMaking event. Rather than sending holiday cards in December, we took Nancy's advice to send greetings for an alternate holiday. WBENC now sends a Valentine to our key corporate contacts, Forum members and vendors—a perfect symbol of our appreciation and passion for our colleagues' success. I was never thanked for sending a Christmas card but have received a great deal of positive response to our Valentine. Recipients have taken the time to e-mail, call or otherwise comment on the card. Black History Month, Women's History Month and other dates can become your branded recognition opportunity.

The goal of all of this networking and meeting and greeting and follow-up, not to mention the certification and marketing we have already explored, is, of course, to secure a meeting with a corporate purchasing official at your top prospect company. Now that you have started to build and maintain your network of contacts, the next chapter begins your step-by-step guide to pitching for, winning and keeping your dream contract.

Success Story: Sharon Evans, president and CEO, CFj Manufacturing

Sharon Evans began manufacturing jewelry and opened a small store in Saginaw, Texas in 1983. In the beginning there were tough times. That first Christmas, Evans was behind 240 custom pieces that customers had ordered as gifts—gifts that, unfortunately, would not make it under the tree. Fortunately, her customers were understanding and she eventually filled all of the orders. "I did not know a lot about manufacturing then. It was quite a learning curve," Evans says.

In the late1980s, Evans added to the jewelry line with lapel pins for large corporations. "One thing led to another and they began asking us for other items, such as service awards and branded promotional products."

In 1996, JCPenney entrusted Evans to handle their service award jewelry program. Evans proved herself—not just on quality, but with outstanding customer service. According to Connie A. Magers, JCPenney's manager of supplier diversity development, "We took a risk in providing her with an opportunity to handle our entire service award program and expand her product line, and she made us proud."

So proud, in fact, that JCPenney began giving Sharon more opportunities and began recommending her to other companies, like Frito-Lay, whose corporate office is across the street from JCPenney in Plano, Texas.

Evans soon realized that the items JCPenney and Frito-Lay were using and requesting were the same for many companies. It did not take long for CFj, under the leadership of Evans, to consolidate orders and reduce prices for other large corporations.

Today, Evans provides JCPenney with an array of products, including custom chocolate candy bars, vinyl hang tags, coffee and break room supplies, gift-with-purchase and purchase-with-purchase items for giveaway and sale, service awards, promotional items and Waterford crystal vases. Magers says, "Whatever we need, Evans always seems to provide it and always delivers on time. Her creativity and energy are what keep us going back to CFj over and over again."

Evans currently has about 160 employees, 125 of whom are in the United States. The company has offices in Fort Worth,

Boston, Chicago, Dallas, Russia, Hong Kong and Israel. The little store in Saginaw still stands.

In January 2004, Evans was invited to the White House to meet with President Bush to discuss the effects of new tax legislation on WBEs, and later that year she attended a White House Christmas party.

In May 2005, Fast Company magazine honored her as number eight on its list of the Top 25 Women Business Builders. She also received accolades from her customers, including the JCPenney National Supplier Diversity Development Award, the Frito-Lay Other Goods & Services Vendor of the Year, the Frito-Lay National Minority/Woman Supplier of the Year and the Boy Scouts of America National Award of Excellence.

Evans is active in WBE issues on the local and national level. She serves on the board of directors for WBENC and recently participated in the recommendation panel for the 2004 search for America's Top Corporations for WBEs. On the local level, she is secretary on the board of directors for the Women's Business Council-Southwest. Evans also volunteers her time to several community organizations and she founded the Small World Children's Foundation, which helps underprivileged children in Peru. She is involved with Olive Branch Ministries, a medical team that provides assistance to underdeveloped countries and her company also created its own scholarship program.

Despite all the success and rewards, Evans is not content to rest on her laurels. She has a plan for her company: "I want us to be the biggest and best at what we do."

Chapter Five

Alternative and Advanced Supplier Strategies

As you continue to build relationships and begin to plan your official sales pitch to corporations, you should consider the various entry points that are available to you. While the most common scenario—and the strategy I have focused on thus far—is for one certified supplier to pursue a contract with one corporate buyer, there are several other possibilities. This chapter outlines a variety of alternative supplier strategies and how to make them work for you.

Why is it important to consider alternative strategies? WBENC's 2003 *Access to Markets Survey* found that an average of only 38 percent of Fortune 1000 Corporations' spending is up for renewal or rebidding each year. Why? Think about trends in the business world today: The pressures of cost-cutting, globalization, vendor consolidation and "bundled" contracts (that consolidate two or more procurement requirements for goods or services previously provided under separate, smaller contracts) have narrowed opportunities to attain new business for GMEs and other suppliers.

Smart business owners change with the times and do what they can to grow, even in a challenging economic environment.

Strategic Alliances

For a variety of reasons, such as size, geographic location or technological limitation, some GMEs are not able to fulfill all requirements of a particular corporate contract. In such cases, a strategic alliance with another GME may be a smart strategy for pitching and winning the business. For our purposes, "strategic alliance" can be defined as a formal business relationship (short of a partnership, merger or acquisition) formed for the purpose of fulfilling a corporate contract that each company could not fulfill on its own.

How exactly does this work? An alliance can comprise two, three or several businesses related in the following ways:

- Vertical Integration – For example, a graphic design firm could partner with a web hosting company to provide full web design and implementation services under one contract. That same graphic designer might partner with a printer whose quality and service matches their own corporate culture, thus providing a corporate client with end-to-end production of brochures and other paper products. Or, all three could join together.

- Horizontal Integration – You can partner with a competitor to increase geographic reach or staff capacity. Two technology staffing firms, for example, might unite to provide staffing in multiple cities rather than just their own. In this way, Company #1 can fulfill the needs of corporations that might be headquartered in that company's region, but which have locations in more than one area of the country, which can be serviced by Company #2.

If you form a new company or partnership, remember to have that entity certified in its own right so that there will be no questions as to its ability to compete within the supplier diversity process. Note that the topic of partnerships and strategic alliances is explored in greater depth in my book, *Partnering for Profit: Success Strategies for Tomorrow's Supply Chain* (published by WBENC, June 2005, through a grant from Manpower Inc.). You can download an order form at *www.wbenc.org*.

Here are some successful examples of strategic alliances:

Lana Shannon and Cindy Wilson

Bruce Perkins, vice president, manager, supplier diversity & business development for Merrill Lynch says that those in corporate America who are truly committed to women and minority entrepreneurship will do whatever they can to help GMEs to succeed. He certainly proved his commitment in the case of Lana Shannon and Cindy Wilson. Bruce had what he describes as a "great relationship" with each of these entrepreneurs, having educated and encouraged both of them about certification. He knew that on their own they might be too small to win business from large companies like Merrill, so he wanted to encourage them to consider strategic alliances. Bruce invited Lana and Cindy as his guests to WBENC's Salute to Women's Business Enterprises gala, where he knew there would be many successful certified businesses in attendance. Both Lana and Cindy took him up on his offer.

Cindy Wilson, owner of Wilson West Inc., an event development and management company in San Francisco, says that when she arrived at the gala and looked at the seating chart, she thought, "Who is strong enough to name her company 'Chicks With Ideas'? I want to sit next to her!" It was Lana Shannon, whose Connecticut-based company produces promotional items. They did sit next to each other and formed a personal connection immediately. The two women turned out to have a lot in common: Both had two kids and, interestingly enough, Cindy had braces on her teeth at the time and Lana was about to get them. After the event, a professional connection formed as well. Lana was looking at a Merrill Lynch RFP involving both promotional items and special events. She suggested an alliance with Cindy and proposed including a third, non-GME partner, Barrington, which could increase their distribution on a national basis.

The three companies joined together and formed the CBW Group (as in, Chicks-Barrington-Wilson). Although they did not win that particular Merrill Lynch contract, the three partners of CBW Group share business with each other frequently, enabling each to cut costs and fuel growth. Both Lana and Cindy still have their own successful individual businesses, but when large RFPs arise, they can pull their strategic alliance out of their "tool chest" and bid for big contracts.

This story again confirms the importance of building strong relationships with supplier diversity professionals and taking advantage of opportunities they present to you. As Bruce Perkins exemplifies, supplier diversity executives can provide you with education, encouragement and essential support in navigating the waters of supplying to large corporate customers.

Cindy and Lana, who clearly understand the importance of networking, are members of the Women Presidents' Organization as well. In 2003 they jointly presented a panel at the WPO National Conference on "Expansion Through Strategic Alliances," which I was proud to moderate.

Systrand and ThyssenKrupp Presta

Like Merrill Lynch, Ford Motor Company assists its suppliers in the formation of strategic alliances. Dr. Ray Jensen, Ford's former director, supplier diversity development, says, "As one of the nation's largest corporations, Ford believes it has an obligation to lead through its actions and motivate through its success. Ford's commitment to supplier diversity is made possible because of the exceptional quality of the goods and services provided by its diverse suppliers." (As mentioned earlier, Ray was so strongly committed to this philosophy that when he retired from Ford at the end of 2005, he joined WBE firm Innovision Technologies as president.)

Armando Ojeda, former president of the United States Hispanic Chamber of Commerce has ably replaced Ray at Ford.

Armando and his team prove their commitment by matching GMEs with some of their largest suppliers. ThyssenKrupp Presta, one of the largest European automotive suppliers, contacted Ford seeking a capable minority- or woman-owned machining company for a potential joint venture. Ford suggested Systrand Manufacturing, a Zenith Group WBE owned by Sharon Cannarsa, because of her company's strong history of quality and its ability to handle more complex machining processes.

Systrand and ThyssenKrupp Presta partnered as suggested and presented an idea for a strategic alliance that would machine camshafts. Ford decided that this was a commodity they would have a significant need for in the future and agreed to support the joint venture if it could provide high quality parts at competitive prices. They did, and Ford awarded three camshaft production contracts to the alliance, which took on the combined name SystrandPresta Engine Systems. Total revenues for the camshaft business are projected to grow to over $100 million by 2007.

Linden International

WBE Mary Kay Hamm, president of Linden International, participated in the Tuck-WBENC Executive Management Program. There she proposed a business idea to program director Len Greenhalgh and an executive from Exelon. But she knew she needed help to make it happen.

"First, I had this idea," Mary Kay explains. She asked Craig Adams, now chief supply officer at Exelon, to mentor her. "He was very helpful and gave me an hour of his time initially. He told me what would make sense and work for him and what would play at Exelon. That guided me and helped me construct the offering, based on WBENC's programs to accelerate the growth of WBEs. Craig had used those programs many times to find and pair WBEs with other companies. He was way out front with this. Exelon is a model of pairing WBEs with each other or with majority-owned firms to make them part of the supply chain."

According to Craig, "Our objective is to try to create partnering relationships where WBE businesses can have different pieces of the business and they can grow as their financial strength and capabilities grow."

The process took a while. "I reapproached Craig every six months or so for two years. Each time I told him, 'We are still interested, we have done this to advance the idea and have the structure in place to support it.' And then I would ask him, 'What is the climate there and what do you think?'"

Eventually the timing was right and Craig Adams and Exelon said yes. The next step was for Linden to form an alliance with the help of Exelon. "I team with a majority-owned company," Mary Kay explains. "I am the project executive and they provide the research. Len Greenhalgh has a strong procurement background and was helpful in explaining how to do strategic partnerships. We knew there was a risk: most do not work. Len was a helpful coach and supporter.

"We wrote a contract with Exelon [and the majority-owned business] to provide strategic sourcing for Exelon and we have just finished the project for them. We evaluate their contracts, put out RFPs and advise them on next steps. We have saved Exelon 4 to 30 percent in the three categories of products they gave us.

Linden's project with Exelon is set up as contingency-based. According to Mary Kay, this means that, "Every dollar that flows through in savings to Exelon flows through to my company. If we save them a dollar, we take a portion and they keep a portion. In this way, they increase their WBE spend without increasing their outlay."

Mary Kay credits much of the success of this strategic alliance to her relationship with Craig Adams. "It worked out because Craig is my corporate champion," She says. "He has known me on the Women Business Development Center/Philadelphia

Board of Directors for five years. I had built a good relationship and he apparently has a high level of trust in me."

How does Craig describe their relationship? "We had ongoing dialogue in regard to her business—computer software support. I listened to what her goals were, and what work she was doing to try to grow her business and explore partnership opportunities. It was about being able to reach out when the right opportunity came to her.

"She has a neat mix of patience and tenacity. It takes both," he says.

The Elements Alliance

Debbie Faraone is a WBE whose company, The Elements, Inc., provides products that reinforce clients' brands. Debbie, already a successful supplier to such large companies as Freddie Mac, began to recognize a void for many of her clients. She wisely realized that combining her talents with other related businesses would provide more value to her existing clients and help her gain new clients:

> "While my core business creates tangible solutions to help organizations power their brand, many times it seemed my clients needed assistance in developing their brand before I could help them bring it to life.
>
> At the same time, I had developed a strong personal and professional relationship with Karen McSteen, president of brandMatters. The more Karen and I talked, the more we realized that there were synergies that existed between our businesses and our business philosophies. In our discussions, the value proposition for an alliance began to emerge. In looking at our respective competencies, we realized that we needed additional expertise in design to make our value proposition complete. We both had experience working with a tremendously

talented designer and asked her to join us as part of the alliance as well."

The three formed The Elements Alliance, a Limited Liability Corporation (LLC) and began to market their services as a group. Although The Elements, Inc. continues to produce its brand-building products, The Elements Alliance can now provide a wider array of services, including brand strategy development, qualitative research, communications and messaging strategy, design, editorial, digital media and creative product reinforcement.

Corporations also benefit from the fact that they can trust The Elements Alliance to work well together and ensure fully integrated brand initiatives across various projects—a result that is not always guaranteed when a company works with a variety of independent vendors.

Debbie's story shows that combining talents is one of the best strategies a GME can use, not only to find new clients, but also to expand business with existing clients.

Cheat Sheet: Forming a Strategic Alliance

How do you find companies interested in an alliance? This cheat sheet offers several strategies to try. Of course you will want to vet potential partners as you would any business partner, but one good sign that they are a viable, strong business is to look for their certification—certification from a respected organization shows that the company has been carefully vetted. And, if you meet a potential partner when you are out networking, you will know right away that the other businessperson understands marketing and networking just like you do!

- Attend events for GMEs – As Lana Shannon and Cindy Wilson's story proves, it is important to show up at events where other successful certified businesses will be in attendance.

- Advertise – Consider placing an ad in your industry newsletter, magazine or listserv, or, as you read earlier, on Google or other search engines.
- Search – Search supplier databases such as WBENCLink for companies in the industry or geographic location in which you are looking to partner.
- Network with other businesses in your industry and learn who is well-respected by your peers.
- Ask your current clients who they use in other regions of the country or for synergistic products and services.
- When you do form an alliance, promote it! Marilyn Bushey, president of Texas-based Power Performance and Communication, Inc., dedicates a page of her website to her strategic alliances. On the page she lists five companies with whom she partners. "PowerPAC has formed this global network of outstanding strategic partners to better service our clients," the headline reads. Then each company's capabilities are described in terms of how each complements PowerPAC's own services.

Informal Referral Networks

If formal strategic alliances are not the right choice for you, you may want to consider an informal vendor referral arrangement. E. Denise Stovell, president of Stovell Marketing and Public Relations, has produced WBENC's Salute to Women's Business Enterprises gala and the Women in Business Conference for several years. While managing the production of invitations, websites and program books, she has been able to evaluate the quality and creativity of many of WBENC's other suppliers who work on these events. Denise has witnessed firsthand their service philosophy and, because she frequently negotiates on WBENC's behalf, their pricing strategies. Through her contract with WBENC, Denise has developed a "stable" of WBE suppliers whose products and services complement her own—and whose staff she trusts and respects. This "insider" knowledge allows Denise to assist any new clients with strategic planning of their events, and enables her to recommend qualified vendors to complement her services. This brings increased credibility to Denise's reputation without ever signing a formal strategic alliance agreement with the other vendors or expanding her staff.

Second Tier Opportunities

Second Tier suppliers are diverse suppliers used as subcontractors by a First Tier (also known as "Prime") supplier to a corporation. Second Tier suppliers generally count toward a company's supplier diversity goals, so it is in a corporation's best interest to ensure that their larger First Tier suppliers meet and do business with smaller Second Tier players, and that the First Tier suppliers report on their usage of diverse subcontractors. Second Tier supplying is yet another door into a corporation, and one that GMEs are increasingly using. I strongly encourage you to consider Second Tier opportunities in your quest to grow your business.

Consider this more detailed definition of Second Tier supplying:

"Second Tier is a function of who is the customer. A First Tier company is a supplier that invoices your company for goods and/or services rendered *directly* by that supplier. A Second Tier supplier is a supplier that invoices a company's First Tier supplier for goods and/or services rendered. The Second Tier process strongly encourages or requires its prime suppliers/contractors to develop a program that engages MWBE in its supply process and encourages the development of MWBE firms."[vi]

Why are Second Tier programs important to corporations and GMEs? As Rutgers University states on its procurement website, "Second Tier sourcing programs have value because, by supporting the growth of minority- and woman-owned business on all levels of the economic food chain, they enhance the economic viability of all business concerns.

"The overall objective is to encourage the development and implement sustainable opportunities for [GMEs] to participate in the customer's procurement processes where it makes economic sense to do so.[vii]

A section on the Wells Fargo supplier diversity website further describes the importance and benefits of Second Tier programs:

> "Second Tier suppliers are subcontractors who provide goods and services to primary Wells Fargo suppliers. This arrangement provides more business opportunities for smaller companies that may not qualify as primary suppliers. By gaining experience as a Second Tier supplier, these vendors can also position themselves to compete for primary supplier opportunities in the future."

Many of America's large corporations highly value Second Tier suppliers. They may be Second Tier, but they are by no means second-class.

In fact, some corporations require all First Tier suppliers to establish diverse spend goals with their subcontractors. Bank of America, for example, provides a supplier diversity orientation with all First Tier suppliers once their contract is implemented, laying out the Bank's expectations with respect to Second Tier goals, certification of subcontractors and Second Tier reporting requirements. To prove its seriousness, Bank of America monitors these Second Tier results on a quarterly basis.

A potential drawback to Second Tier corporate supplying, however, is that the onus for creating opportunities and reporting results often falls on the First Tier supplier, whose programs are often not as developed or as well-monitored as Fortune 500 corporate supplier diversity programs. This means that you must remain diligent and remind your First Tier company to report your contribution to any contracts in which you participate. Remember, particularly if the First Tier supplier is not a GME, you are bringing enormous value as a diverse business. They need you.

How can you make your Second Tier status known to the corporation receiving the benefit of your services? One suggestion is to offer to help the First Tier supplier complete the paperwork reporting required by a corporation. Another tactic, as suggested by Heather Herndon Wright, whose additional suggestions appear in this section's "Cheat Sheet," is to offer to accompany your First Tier supplier on sales calls. This ensures that the corporation knows a GME is involved in the contract, and, of course, it helps you build a relationship with the end user.

Cheat Sheet: How to Become a Second Tier Supplier

To become a Second Tier supplier you will need to implement many of the same marketing and networking strategies you have been using to reach corporate buyers. Heather Herndon Wright, president and CEO of Herndon-Wright Enterprises, offers some specific pointers from her experience on both sides of the table—as former national director of supply chain diversity at Lucent and a current WBE:

- Never bypass the chance to perform at a Second Tier level if it is suggested to you by your supplier diversity contacts. You are not giving up your relationship with your customer;

you are just serving his or her needs in a different way.

- Remember, however, that corporate buyers are often very busy and overwhelmed, so they are not always thinking about where you might fit in their supply chain. You need to come to them with "out of the box" solutions. Educate your customers on exactly what you can provide and work with them to identify multiple points of entry into their supply chain so you can operate most effectively.

- Actively market yourself as a Second Tier supplier as part of your pitch to corporations. Immediately look for indirect ways to supply them in any capacity you can. This is particularly important in today's environment of outsourced procurement or when a corporation is seeking a global, multi-product contract. Can your business fulfill a particular regional need, or supply a niche product?

- Do not be afraid to market yourself to your competitors. Larger competitors may be able to include your business as a Second Tier supplier in a large contract with an existing customer. In addition, this could result in a great way for you expand your customer base and supply your products or services to additional companies already being served by your competitor.

- Show your value to the First Tier suppliers. If you are a reliable, high-quality Second Tier supplier, chances are the Prime will partner with you again on other contracts.

- Do not stop at Second Tier—look at Third, Fourth, and on down the line. There may be several points of entry for various product and service offerings in a single contract.

- View your Second Tier status as an opportunity to be mentored by the First Tier company. As a Second Tier supplier you are gaining additional experience to provide more value as a Prime supplier.

While we are on the subject of Second Tier supplying: Do you have a supplier diversity program for your company? If not, you should. No matter at what point you enter the supply chain, your diversity dollars not only help your customer's reporting needs and goals, but also increase your own credibility. Furthermore, you can use your own diversity initiative as a marketing tool when you approach that corporate buyer or First Tier company.

Leslie Saunders of Leslie Saunders Insurance and Marketing derives an extraordinary fifty percent of her business from other WBEs. In turn, she uses other WBEs as suppliers. "My broker for my employee benefits is a WBE," she says, "And I have a woman attorney, and my trade show booth was made by a WBENC member, as were my holiday cards, my promotional materials, etc. And any time we go to Office Depot we make sure our files say 'Smead.'[Smead Manufacturing is led by WBE Sharon Avent.] Whenever possible, I will use a supplier from WBENC. When we work with each other, good things happen. I think that there are a lot of opportunities for WBENC businesses to do business with each other."

Become a Business Solution Partner

Corporations are always on the lookout for seamless service, and one way for smaller GMEs to break into the supply chain is to make it your business to package the skills, products or logistics of several other companies. By integrating an entire solution and offering several services in one package, you make life easier for a corporate buyer who does not want 20 relationships requiring 20 invoices and 20 phone calls a day.

Joan Kerr of AT&T shares the story of WBE Katherine McConvey of KMM Telecommunications. KMM is a business solution partner with large cable manufacturing companies that do not want to bother with the business of managing cable inventory, cutting giant reels of cable to required sizes, re-reeling, warehousing, shipping and tracking them for end users. Katherine has made a business of understanding and delivering all of these logistics. She buys the cable from the large companies, provides the additional services, procures cable stubs for the cut cable from entirely different companies and then offers one-stop shopping for corporate customers that previously had to work with several different companies during the process. KMM is much smaller than her cable industry partners, but she has found a way to play a vital role in the supply chain of large corporations.

Pursue Multiple Corporate Relationships

One interesting practice WBENC discovered when researching our 2002 "Next Practices: Excellence in Corporate Purchasing" report involved TXU Energy. When TXU recognized outsourcing opportunities that one of its *customers* had available, the company identified a WBE with whom to partner to fulfill the opportunity. In other words, TXU formed a strategic alliance with a WBE in order to win a contract for itself. If the particular WBE had not been on TXU's radar screen, she would never have known about this opportunity. Being open to such alternative tactics ultimately results in more business for everyone.

Billie Bryant, president and CEO of CESCO and WBENC Board Member, has an incredible success story of winning contracts through subcontracting. Billie's story demonstrates the values of patience and building relationships to achieve big results. Always seeking new business, Billie became aware of two large bundled RFPs from the Dallas Independent School District (DISD)—one for office supplies and the other for office equipment with some consulting services included. She knew that her company could participate in both RFPs by partnering with larger corporations. Her door to opportunity involved promoting herself as a Second Tier supplier whose WBE status could help larger companies win the contracts.

Billie decided to contact the DISD to educate them on the utilization of GMEs and the importance of the District's supporting local businesses. It did not hurt that Billie could say that her business and her home both supported the District in taxes each year, and that she graduated three sons from the Dallas School System. (Indeed, a good lesson to use what you have got!)

Billie personally visited DISD to share a presentation on supplier diversity, educating them on the value of her small business in partnership with any large supplier. Next, she called some of the large companies that attended the pre-bid meeting to sell her services. According to Billie, it is very important that the large companies understand all the value-added services that a small business can bring to a large bundled contract. It is also very important that technology be among those value-added skills. On the supply side of the RFP, Billie eventually formed an alliance with Office Depot and Corporate Express.

To address the equipment proposal, she had an existing partnership with Xerox dealing with major corporations in facilities management and equipment. However, one of her main contacts at Xerox, Tracey Whitaker, had since retired and was working for Kinko's. When Tracey evaluated the DISD RFP for Kinko's, he remembered working with CESCO and contacted Billie for a potential strategic alliance. Tracey pulled together a team including a few GMEs and the group won the business. As you can see, strong relationships last even when supplier diversity professionals change companies.

In the end, the DISD director of purchasing thanked Billie for educating the District on how smaller GME businesses can work with large suppliers and Billie realized her goal of participating in both large bundled contracts. Billie used her commitment, contacts and hard work to form valuable alliances to service large customers.

Matchmaker, Matchmaker, Make Me a Match...

Is your head spinning yet? I know it can be overwhelming to consider all of the options from prime contracts to strategic alliances to Second, Third and Fourth Tier supplier relationships. Sometimes certified businesses can feel like they have too many decisions to make. This, again, is where the supplier diversity community—certification organizations in particular—demonstrates its true commitment to your success and the success you can bring to America's corporations.

Enter matchmaking.

WBENC, the NMSDC, our affiliates and our corporate members provide "connecting" resources to help you find the right fit with the right partners for your business. WBENC's MatchMaker Meeting Series, for example, connects WBENC-certified WBEs with corporate purchasing officials for private face-to-face meetings to discuss potential opportunities.

WBENC's listserv, *WBENC-Discuss@wbenc.org*, notifies all certified WBEs of upcoming MatchMaker meetings. WBEs apply to attend these meetings by completing a "WBE Profile Sheet" and application attached to the notification e-mail for each specific MatchMaker meeting in which they wish to participate. These forms are then used by the MatchMaker corporation's purchasing personnel, along with a supplier's WBENCLink profile, in the selection process. (Yet another reason to make sure your WBENC profile—and any online profile—is always current!) Attendees are then selected for this mega-opportunity to meet with corporations *that have pre-selected you.*

Audrey Goins Brichi of Chevron's supplier diversity program highly recommends MatchMaker meetings to GMEs wanting to do business with her company. "The best way to approach Chevron is through direct contact at an event designed specifically for matchmaking," she says. "In that situation, Chevron and the business owner are focused on the same objective: creating a winning partnership that drives value for both of our companies. We both benefit from an in-person conversation where critical questions can be answered up front."

Cheat Sheet: WBENC MatchMaker Meeting Program Timeline

While matchmaker programs can vary from organization to organization, the program timeline for a WBENC MatchMaker event provides insight into how the process works:

Stated Goal: The goal of the MatchMaker Program is to pair WBENC-certified women business enterprises (WBEs) and corporate purchasing officials for private one-on-one meetings to discuss business opportunities.

Each corporation participating in a MatchMaker event works differently and the structure of the event varies, so we tailor a schedule to meet a corporation's individual needs.

8 WEEKS OUT
* WBEs receive announcement notices via WEBuy@wbenc.org, WBENC's e-mail listserv dedicated to sourcing opportunities.

7 WEEKS OUT
* Reminder notice sent via WEBuy@wbenc.org. WBEs are encouraged to submit their profiles as early as possible.
* WBENC vets WBE applications to confirm that the WBE is certified with WBENC and may do additional screening per the agreement with the corporation (location of business in a specific geographic region, etc.).

6 WEEKS OUT
* Deadline for submission of WBE profiles for those interested in participating in the MatchMaker event.
* Corporation begins review of profiles and selection of WBEs.

4 WEEKS OUT

- Selected WBEs are sent notice about their participation in the MatchMaker meeting. Corporation must notify WBENC of non-buyer appointments, such as appointments with supplier diversity managers. This information is passed along to the WBE selected.

3 1/2 WEEKS OUT

- Final notices sent to WBEs selected to participate in the program. WBEs not selected for the MatchMaker are also notified. While it is not always possible, due to the length of a corporation's decision-making process, we strive to provide a minimum of three weeks notice so that WBEs can get the best possible rate for their travel and hotel accommodations.

2 WEEKS OUT

- Deadline for selected WBEs to confirm their availability to participate in the MatchMaker meeting.
- Appointment times scheduled with specific corporate representative(s) and WBE.
- Confirmation e-mails with specifics on the event and appointment times are sent to the selected WBEs.

Are matchmaker meetings for everyone? As with any other business opportunity, conduct a cost-benefit analysis to make certain that this is an appropriate opportunity for you and your business. While there is no fee to participate in a MatchMaker meeting, you will be responsible for covering all of your own costs for travel and any other expenses you incur for the presentation.

Making the Most of a Matchmaker Meeting

The advanced strategy of matchmaker meetings is a serious endeavor. You must be thoroughly prepared for both the meeting itself and the possible doors it might open quickly. Here are some important tips:

- Be prepared before you get on the plane and make certain that all of your materials are current and that you are in a position to fulfill any contract that you may be discussing. Even though a matchmaker meeting is not a "formal" presentation, you should develop presentation materials that tell your company's story and that can be left behind with the corporate representative.
- Find out beforehand how much time will be allotted to each meeting and craft your "pitch" accordingly. Do not start a one-hour presentation if you only have twenty minutes. (See the next chapter for more suggestions on planning and executing your sales pitch.)
- Take the time to attend the meeting yourself, even if your vice president of business development normally makes new business calls. Your presence adds weight.
- Be on time. There is never an excuse for tardiness.
- Show up if you scheduled an appointment. At a recent WBENC MatchMaker, two WBE firms that had been selected to participate never showed up and never called. They will *never* have the opportunity to do business with the corporation, or to participate in another WBENC MatchMaker. Do not apply if you do not plan on attending.
- While corporations make every effort to make certain you are matched with the correct person in the company, do your own research and evaluate the specific opportunity with your own cost-benefit analysis. Do not be afraid to ask if there is someone else you might meet with while you are in town.

- Manage your expectations and view the meeting as the beginning of a relationship, not an all-or-nothing event.
- Try to schedule meetings with other current or potential clients in the same geographic location where you are attending a matchmaker meeting to maximize your time.
- Follow up with a thank you letter and additional information, no matter the result of the one-on-one meeting. At the very least, a matchmaker meeting is a great way to make a new connection in a prospect corporation.

WBE and Zenith Group member Mercedes LaPorta, president of Mercedes Electric Supply, Inc., has certainly made the most of the MatchMaker opportunities she has received through WBENC. In preparation for the 2005 WBENC national conference in Las Vegas, Mercedes requested a MatchMaker meeting with MGM Properties.

"I was able to meet with the head of the diversity department at the MatchMaker meeting," Mercedes explains, "but also, thanks to WBENC's help, set up a couple of meetings with the buyers beforehand—for MGM's properties New York, New York and Treasure Island."

Mercedes used her MatchMaker opportunity to demonstrate her capabilities and relevant experience to MGM:

"When I had my meeting I had my company information with me and explained what exactly it is that I have done. I have supplied the electric materials for the Ritz Carlton in Key Biscayne and for the JW Marriott in Miami. This showed that I was familiar with hotels and the electric materials they would need to buy. I had a portfolio of 27 years of projects! I also demonstrated the fact that I had been doing business on a national level before, with Office Depot. I was also able to relay to them I had done a project in Las Vegas. They got a pretty good view [of my ability to handle their business]."

After the success of the MatchMaker meeting, Mercedes followed up with her diversity contact, who put her in touch with MGM's construction department. Mercedes Electric has since started to do business with New York New York, MGM Mirage and the MGM Grand in Las Vegas.

In addition to WBENC, the U.S. Hispanic Chamber of Commerce provides one-on-one matchmaking for businesses. This program is held in conjunction with the Chamber's fall conference. For more information, go to *www.ushcc.com/news-convention.html.*

The U.S. Small Business Administration also conducts a series of business matchmaking conferences throughout the United States in conjunction with the U.S. Chamber of Commerce. Visit *www.sba.gov* for information on this and other one-on-one opportunities presented at these events. The SBA program offers multiple appointments with representatives of both the private sector and government agencies. An online registration system puts you in the driver's seat to determine which agencies and companies you are targeting, but the downside of this arrangement is that the companies and agencies have not pre-selected you (as they do with WBENC's MatchMaker series), so there may not be a match. Honest evaluation of your research is a key to a successful event for you and your company. To find more matchmaker opportunities, research additional associations and organizations.

New to the matchmaking arena are Internet-based trade shows. For Internet trade shows, both corporations and GMEs pay a fee to create an online "booth" that is live on the Internet for anywhere from a few days to a few weeks. Phone and web-based appointments are scheduled in conjunction with the "show." A significant advantage of this approach is that many buyers who do not have the time or budget to travel to physical business fairs can access you and your "booth" over an extended period of time, increasing the likelihood that they will have the time to review your materials. This concept is still developing and the long-term benefits have not yet been evaluated fully, but Internet trade shows are growing in popularity and should be considered as yet another occasion to form relationships with corporate supplier diversity professionals and buyers. For more information, you may want to visit *www.itradefair.com*.

I hope that this chapter has opened your eyes to the many possible "doors" through which you can gain access to corporate contracts. Now that you know your audience (or audiences), it is time get out there and show your stuff. Get ready for your Big Pitch.

Chapter Six

The First "P" of Supplier Diversity Success: PREPARATION for the Big Meeting and Beyond

In the previous chapters you have identified potential corporate customers, honed your marketing messages and networked your way to relationships with supplier diversity professionals and potential strategic partners. You may even have experienced a one-on-one matchmaker meeting with a supplier diversity executive from a prospect company. Now it is time to prepare to take your message beyond the supplier diversity department and directly to the division of the company you will supply.

Remember that supplier diversity professionals—the primary targets of your attention thus far—do not usually make purchasing decisions. In many companies they exercise a strong influence on the process, and in some companies, all final contracts must have the sign-off of the supplier diversity executive, but they are not the only decision makers.

This chapter helps you identify the decision makers for your particular product or service, then advises you on the important topics of pricing and technology, both of which will be crucial to your ultimate pitch. For our purposes in this chapter, I will focus on making one pitch to one company, although it is quite likely you will be pursuing business with more than one company at a time.

Update Your Data

In Chapter Three you learned the fundamental marketing strategy of registering with the supplier databases of all potential corporate customers. If you have not done this already, you must make sure not only that you are registered in the supplier database of the company you are actively pursuing, but also that your file is completely up-to-date. Various decision makers may look up your file, so be sure the information they will find is current, persuasively presented and accurate.

Note that many corporations use a third party portal for their supplier databases. WBENC has found that, of the 20 percent of Fortune 1000 companies that require their suppliers to be e-commerce enabled, the majority (over 60 percent) require that their suppliers create a supplier account on a third party or industry portal, rather than a proprietary system developed by the corporation itself. One of the most popular is Ariba. Many corporations, such as Johnson & Johnson, AT&T and Merrill Lynch, require suppliers to register on the Ariba supplier network to facilitate e-requisitioning and e-invoicing. In addition to Ariba, other e-procurement platforms you may come across include Commerce One, i2 Technologies and Frictionless.

In addition to checking your profile in the corporation's database (or its third party platform), take time now to make sure that your company website is up-to-date and fully functional (now is the time to replace those "Coming Soon!" pages with actual content). Your live presentation is only one step in the pitch process; corporate executives may look for information about you and your business in a variety of places when they are assessing you.

Find Out Who Makes the Decisions

When you have a carefully developed relationship with your supplier diversity contact, he or she will likely introduce you to the proper office within the company. All you will need to do is ask for an introduction to the purchaser (or purchasers) you want to meet. (If you feel you do not have strong support from a corporate supplier diversity professional, go back to Chapters Three and Four, or contact your local Women's Business Organization Partner (WBOP), Regional Minority Council or other GME organization for support and guidance.)

Spotlight: It Helps to Have Friends

Barbara Woyak, owner of Future Trend Technology Management, a WBEC-West certified WBE, received a contract with General Dynamics as a direct result of her WBE certification and the excellent relationship she developed with supplier manager, Ron Steele. When General Dynamics held a special event for diversity suppliers, Ron invited Barbara so she could meet the hiring managers in the company's Information Technology department. Shortly thereafter, Future Trend Technology Management was awarded a contract with General Dynamics. Ron Steele's invitation to Barbara to meet key decision makers opened a big opportunity she might not have found without internal corporate support.

Corporations have various ways of contracting for goods and services, so you are likely to be directed to one of four places:

1. **Formal Corporate Procurement RFP (Request for Proposal) Process:** Formal, competitive sourcing processes are common for large-scale goods and services such as industrial equipment, technology purchases and construction projects. For some firms, all commodities and services are purchased through RFPs, but the company may also perform a "sources sought" or "request for information" to develop lists of potential suppliers. As mentioned above, you must

completely fill out the online or paper database question-naire to even get into the game.

Then you will need to respond to the RFP with a formal written proposal, price quotes and other requested information. As a certified business you will have the advantage of an advocate in the supplier diversity department who can advise you on the preparation of your proposal. Take full advantage of this assistance, as it may prove to be the deciding factor in winning the contract. Everyone likes to be part of a winning team. If you can enlist the supplier diversity executive as a member of your team, you will help to make certain that your response is given appropriate consideration.

All companies will exercise "due diligence" on RFP responses to make certain your business has the capacity to deliver on time and in budget. The larger the opportunity, the more information about your business, its finances and reputation (through references), will be required. Make certain all of your company's documentation is in good shape and complete when you respond to an RFP. Your proposal might not be considered if it is incomplete.

2. **Commodity Managers**: Large manufacturers, such as those in the automotive industry, will utilize purchasing specialists who are expert in a narrow area. This system can expedite your identification of the correct "buyer," but may limit the creative inclusion of your product elsewhere in the company. Do not be afraid to ask for a referral to another commodity manager if you believe there is an opportunity elsewhere in the same corporation. You may have found from networking within your trade association that you can identify commodity managers specific to your industry.

As discussed in Chapter Five, you should also ask if a referral to an existing prime supplier would be a good strategy for you and your business at this point. Recently, I was speaking with a senior executive of an Asian-owned business who informed me that the company had just landed a $1 billion, three-year contract with IBM. Part of their challenge in complying with the contract requirements was that they needed to identify diverse subcontractors within their commodity area for their Second Tier goals. I invited them to use *WEBuy@wbenc.org* to identify WBEs that could be of assistance in fulfilling their subcontracting goals, and I also invited the commodity manager to search WBENCLink for appropriate certified WBEs.

3. **Central Purchasing Offices**: Everyday business materials used by several departments in a corporation, such as office supplies, printing, furniture and paper, are often procured through central buying offices. Generally, the corporation will enter into multi-year contracts for a "bundle" of products or services—a great opportunity for strategic alliances or Second Tier. Each company is different, so research whether your product or service, be it rubber bands or human resources, is purchased department-by-department or through a central purchasing group.

4. **Decentralized Purchasing:** In addition to the more formal buying decisions mentioned above (and depending on corporate policy), departmental managers may be individual employees who are responsible for purchasing decisions that will only affect their department or regional office. Frequently, there will be a dollar cap on such authority. Note that many corporations have switched back and forth between centralized purchasing and decentralized purchasing, so keep your research up-to-date. Do not assume that when your current contract expires that you will be negotiating with the same official you dealt with last time around. Locally based purchasers generally procure such things as staffing services, trainers, local caterers and printers, but each company is different so DO YOUR RESEARCH.

Secure a Meeting With the Decision Makers

Whether you are interested in a First or Second Tier opportunity, you need to follow a logical, well-thought-out process to obtain a meeting with the decision maker who is open to your sales pitch. Just follow this simple Who, When, What and Where strategy:

Who: As mentioned above, work with your corporate supplier diversity contact to set up a meeting with the key decision maker(s) affecting procurement of your product or service. At every stage of the process, keep your supplier diversity contact in the loop. Never "go around" your original contact at a company. If you step on toes, you may risk losing not only this deal, but future opportunities.

When you do arrange a meeting with the decision maker, call your original contact a few days ahead of time to reconfirm exactly who will be in the room. Try to obtain the title and bio for each person so you will be fully prepared. Ideally your supplier diversity contact will provide the bios, or you can search the company website or Google.com for information. The more you know about the people you are pitching (areas of expertise, associations they belong to, previous organizations they have worked for), the better you can form a personal connection during your pitch.

Also consider who will be on your side of the table. Will you bring staff? Strategic partners? I do not advise arriving with an entourage, but a few key staff members may be appropriate, depending on the size and complexity of the contract you are pursuing. Always inform the corporation of how many people will be attending, so they are not caught by surprise when you do not arrive alone.

Always remember that *you*, the business owner, need to attend crucial pitch meetings as well. WBE Sandi Wietzel of the 25-employee firm Marketing Images, Inc., learned this lesson in her outreach efforts to the corporate marketing executives who procure her company's services: "One of the things we have found in marketing our services is that I need to be involved. We used to spend time having people in the sales role going to a lot of events and we expended budget money for them to fly out of town to events and trade shows. And the feedback is that it did not work as well. We found that when I have gone to the events and participated in the presentations and process when we are getting access to marketing individuals, they really appreciate that our company is really buying in from the top down. They seem to feel reassured that they will be able to pick up the phone and call me and I am working through all of the details with them. Then we establish a day-to-day contact person."

Your involvement is not just good practice for getting the sale, but for keeping and growing the business. According to Sandi, "It helps the staff with their relationships—I communicate at one level and they communicate at mid-management level. It makes for a stronger overall team…and it helps me to be involved. It helps me to keep a pulse on what is going on in the organization and anticipate what the client's needs are."

When: You need to set up your meetings according to the purchasing timetable of the company, which, unfortunately, does not always match your desired time frame. Again, work with your supplier diversity or WBOP connections to determine the best time of year to make your pitch.

When considering timing for your pitch, think carefully about your existing capabilities. You must go into the pitch fully capable of managing any work that may arise from the meeting. I cannot overemphasize the danger of overpromising. If you do not feel adequately prepared to fulfill a corporate contract if you receive one, do not set up a meeting that might result in work.

What: Call and speak to the decision makers with whom you will meet about expectations for the meeting. Working with your supplier diversity contact, determine how much time you will have to make your presentation and how much information the meeting attendees will be expecting. You should certainly prepare for any possibility, but it is always helpful to have realistic expectations for what will be accomplished in the meeting and how long you will have to present. It is always better to err on the side of gathering too much information than too little.

Where: It is most likely you will need to travel to the location of the corporate decision maker. Include this time and cost in your planning.

Finally, Linda Steward, president of the Women's Business Enterprise Council - Southeast, reminds GMEs never to show up unannounced at the offices of a corporate supplier diversity executive or a purchaser—even if you happen to be in the neighborhood. Business pitches should always be formally scheduled events.

Carefully Consider Your Pricing

When I was a manufacturers' representative I sold to several different types of customers from small neighborhood shops, to multi-store chains, to mass merchandisers. Pricing was based on the number of locations and the size of each order. Similarly, when you are supplying to corporations or prime contractors, your pricing will need adjusting, so be prepared to negotiate down.

While you are certainly the expert on the pricing of your products or services, keep in mind the following factors when preparing to discuss price with a potential corporate buyer:

- First and foremost, understand what it takes for you to make a profit while you are expanding your market. There is absolutely no point selling to any new customer if you are going to lose money doing so. If you are Wal-Mart, you can afford the occasional loss leader to get people into your store, but smaller companies (and pretty much everyone is smaller than Wal-Mart!) cannot afford to do business at a loss. You should have a very clear understanding of your price structure and the marginal benefit you accrue from your own vendors in servicing larger quantity orders, so that you will know exactly how low you can go in a contract negotiation before you ever set foot in the door to pitch a corporation. Be conservative in your budgeting, and I highly recommend meeting with your accountant or financial manager before discussing price with any corporate buyer.

- Be aware of the standards in your industry. Do as much research as you can (through networking, industry associations and conversations with your supplier diversity contacts) to make sure you are in the same ballpark—or even lower-priced—than your competition.

- If you charge more than your competitors, be prepared to explain why. For instance, do you have newer technology or offer different quantities?

- Think about how time consuming it will be to work with this particular client. For both service and product-based businesses, high maintenance clients can eat up your time and your staff's time, and as we all know, time is money. If possible, speak to a company's current suppliers in order to (tactfully) assess how demanding a client they may be; then set your prices accordingly.

- Consider new ways to cut your costs or improve your cash flow in order to pass the savings on to your corporate customer. You might think about offering a discount if the customer pays an invoice within ten days; requiring custom orders to be paid up front; or even moving your warehousing closer to the customer to save on trucking costs. Again, look to the standards in your industry for discounting and cost-cutting ideas.

- Service businesses should also consider implementing quantity discounts. Think about it: If your corporate customer is going to buy 100 times the number of hours that your sales training company normally provides per customer, consider the fact that you will now have lower marketing costs because you are doing business with one customer rather than 100 separate customers. There is also only one company to bill and one invoice to send. You benefit from the bulk sale as much as your customer because you save on these costs and others, and you can (and should) pass this savings on to your customer as part of your contract negotiation.

For more help planning your pricing strategy, consult your professional association for comparative information about your particular field.

Everything You Need to Know About Technology...But Were Too Busy Checking Your E-mail to Ask

In today's fast-moving, competitive, global economy, technology plays a key role in any business relationship, and therefore will be addressed in any serious discussion about working with a large corporation. It is essential that you are prepared for the technological aspect of supplying corporate America, particularly as you prepare to make your sales pitch to decision makers.

As you read through the following advice, I urge you to view technology knowledge and execution as marketing tools, competitive advantages and essential costs of doing business.

The technological aspect of servicing corporate America can be very challenging and potentially expensive, but the investment of time, energy and resources is worth the reward.

Specific requirements vary widely depending on your industry, the company you are pitching, the amount of business you will be contracting for and the complexity of your product or service. Therefore, for this section I have gathered recommendations from a diverse group of GMEs, consultants and corporate executives on the topics most frequently discussed regarding technology.

Ten Technology Tips

Technology Tip #1: Technology is essential to servicing corporate America.

Technology cannot be avoided, so you may as well learn to love it. I certainly have—I carried the entire draft of this book on a tiny "jump drive" (also known as a thumb drive) that hangs from my keychain and plugs into the USB port of my computer! I also frequently download my e-mail while on the road at wireless Internet sites at coffee shops and in airport lounges (as I wait to use the boarding passes I printed from the Internet), or I read e-mail messages directly on my cell phone.

If you are new to the world of technology, remember that, no matter what your age or interest level, technology is not something to be feared. If you feel uncomfortable, sign up for a continuing education class or hire an IT consultant to show you the ropes. WBE Pamela Chambers O'Rourke, president of Icon Information Consultants, LP, reminds beginners that you do not need to know how to install, run and fix every software program on the market, but you do need to understand the basics for your industry. Just as you would not enter a meeting with a potential client without an understanding of the core finances of your business, do not enter a meeting without knowing—and being able to discuss—your company's technological capabilities.

According to Joan Kerr of AT&T, the most important point for GMEs regarding technology is to understand and adapt to the way in which large corporations, and those companies in your industry in particular, do business through technology. From basic e-mail to sophisticated Customer Relationship Management (CRM) software, electronic enablement ("e-enablement") is driven by a corporation's never-ending need for efficiency, quality and economy. So, show that your company possesses the technology to service them in the most high-quality, efficient and economical way. Make it easy for a company to work with you by matching your systems to their needs.

Technology Tip #2: Different companies have different requirements. Ask.

Before you panic and spend a lot of money on new technology, find out what exactly is required to do business with the corporation you are pursuing. According to WBENC's 2001 *Corporate Benchmarking Survey*, only 20 percent of companies *require* that all of their suppliers, including GMEs, be e-commerce capable. How can you find out if your corporate prospects require a certain type of technology? Ask! This should be part of *your* due diligence process—not theirs.

Also remember that technology requirements can change frequently, so keep yourself up-to-date on the varying needs of your customers. Nikki Olyai of Innovision Technologies strongly encourages GMEs to communicate with corporate contacts about their current *and* future technology requirements for suppliers. "Proactive information and data gathering from the client will provide you with a competitive advantage in developing your technology infrastructure," she says. The more you know, the better you can determine which companies you can service and the more specific and persuasive sales presentation you can make.

Nikki also points out that corporate technology plans and requirements are often considered proprietary information and are held confidential. Therefore, it is recommended that you offer to sign a non-disclosure agreement (NDA) or other confidentiality agreement to ensure that you will have access to this information. Processes vary depending on the company you are pursuing, so again, it is always best to ask about specific policies and procedures.

Billie Bryant adds that the buyer or supplier diversity executive may actually *not* be the best person to provide technological information or advice on your bid, especially if you provide a high tech product or service. You may need to do some digging in the company to speak to more technologically-involved corporate employees. But, as Billie points out, this additional research helps you build even more relationships in your corporate customer's company.

Technology Tip #3: Be honest about your technological knowledge and capabilities.

When you are in discussions with a corporation, be up front about your knowledge and capabilities—or lack thereof—regarding technology. As Pamela Chambers O'Rourke advises, "Whatever you tell the client you are going to do, do it. Or, be honest about the fact that you cannot." It is very rare that a company will turn away a supplier who does not have a certain piece of technology, as long as the supplier is willing to acquire the technology to carry out the contract.

As with every other element of your business, never over-promise when it comes to technology. You can destroy a relationship by failing to deliver, or worse, by ruining a project because you did not use technology properly.

Technology Tip #4: Take every opportunity to improve.

Feel like your technology knowledge leaves something to be desired? Pamela Prince-Eason, senior director, Global Sourcing, Pfizer, points out that you can often educate yourself on the Internet. For instance, she says, "If you are proficient with Microsoft Word, PowerPoint and Excel, but you have never used a flowcharting tool, you can probably learn this program in one sitting on the Internet. You can download a tutorial for almost anything these days."

Billie Bryant was lucky enough to have one of her corporate customers, TXU, invite her to its headquarters several years ago to view their plans to move their procurement process to an Electronic Data Interchange (EDI) system (see more on EDI, below). Billie immediately purchased the software (for which the corporation negotiated a special rate for its suppliers), knowing that it was an important investment. "Take advantage of any opportunities corporations present to their vendor base regarding electronic purchasing," Billie counsels. "Be willing to purchase the necessary software, but know that it will probably not be the last new software you have to purchase!" In fact, this same corporation gave CESCO an additional opportunity to build an online marketplace for e-commerce procurement. Even though this required additional resources from CESCO, the new technology resulted in increased revenue for the company. In addition, it gave CESCO the capabilities to perform for other large corporations.

Likewise, take advantage of technology workshops offered at conferences or seminars sponsored by corporations or regional certification organizations. These educational opportunities can be even more helpful than community college or adult education classes because they are specifically targeted to GMEs wanting to do business with corporate America.

Technology Tip #5: E-mail rules.

At the very least, every GME must have an Internet connection and e-mail proficiency. Since applying for certification requires the same minimum requirement, I will assume that you have this one covered, and that e-mail accounts for a large portion of your daily communication.

It is truly amazing how much business is now conducted via e-mail. Think back only a few decades ago when most business was conducted on the local, face-to-face level. Now, virtually any business can compete virtually anywhere (pun intended!). For instance, Joan Kerr of AT&T has interacted almost entirely over e-mail with the production company providing music for her company's supplier diversity achievement awards ceremony. The producers sent proposed audio clips via e-mail, allowing Joan and her team to review the music quickly and provide feedback to incorporate instantaneously. Not only is this pretty cool, it saves everyone time and money by eliminating the production cost of CDs or tapes and the expense of overnight shipping back and forth.

Additional e-mail tips include:

- I do think it is important to remind all GMEs—all businesspeople, in fact—to regularly check your e-mail, or have someone on your staff check it for you. Do not let an important message from a corporation get lost in an overflowing e-mail inbox. During the writing of this book, WBENC was able to take advantage of "remainder" space in a magazine to run an advertisement for our national conference at no cost because my assistant checked my e-mail while I was out of the office. (Now I can actually check my email myself on my Treo cell phone—and many business owners today have Treos or BlackBerries—but sometimes I find it convenient to let my assistant follow up directly.)
- Check that your e-mail account has enough memory to

handle large file attachments, such as PowerPoint presentations, graphic layouts, spreadsheets and, of course, audio clips. It is unprofessional and poor customer service to say that a file is too large for your system to handle. If necessary, speak with your IT department or an IT consultant to expand your account capacity. This is particularly crucial for artistic businesses such as graphic designers, writers and film/video producers.

- Make sure all of your marketing materials and other important documents are e-mailable. Pamela Chambers O'Rourke, whose corporate customers include such large companies as ConocoPhillips, HP, Pitney Bowes, Shell and Waste Management, says that she sends all of her marketing materials and presentation materials to her customers via e-mail. "I find that the 'soft' copies I send via e-mail do not get deleted, whereas paper copies often get thrown away."

- Speaking of databases, always keep yours 100 percent up-to-date. If your company runs on a network with many users, be sure that an update entered by one of your staff members can be accessed by all users. Synchronize everything and back up everything.

Technology Tip #6: Never skimp on security.

Old economy or new economy, corporations must rely on their suppliers for business continuity under any circumstances. This means that, even with "simple" technologies such as Microsoft Word documents and e-mail messages, security is of paramount concern. Pamela Prince-Eason, specifically points out the importance of security in the areas listed below. Although many of these issues appear to be common sense, they are worth mentioning when you outline your capabilities to a potential customer:

- Revision management on written documents, such as the "Track Changes" function on Microsoft products. This is crucial when presentations, documents and contracts are shared back and forth from corporation to supplier. Every change must be accounted for.
- Archiving of documents. Save every draft of every document.
- Disaster recovery and disaster contingency. Do you have a backup system in place? And, if your business is primarily electronic, could you do your job manually in case of disaster?
- Password protection. As CEO, make sure none of your employees can access your confidential files, especially if you operate on a shared network.

WBENC's WBENCLink Internet database proved helpful after 2005's Katrina and Rita hurricanes. While Women's Business Council Gulf Coast Executive Director Kate Chrisman had relocated from New Orleans to Birmingham, Alabama, she was able to download a list of businesses with contact information. WBEs either temporarily or permanently cut off from business documents at their place of business were able to download some of this important information from their stored online application in the WBENCLink database. Importantly, they and their customers could download a .pdf file of their WBE certificate, a new technology launched by WBENC in 2004.

Beyond WBENC, web-based storage sites for everything from family photos to legal records are becoming increasingly available and are worth investigation.

Technology Tip #7: The trend toward third party purchasing portals will continue.

As you learned earlier, many companies use third party supplier portals such as Ariba to find and transact with suppliers. Ariba is the most commonly used portal at the moment, but other providers offer comparable services. Remember, you may register on one or many third party platforms as part of your marketing process, or you may be requested to sign up by a corporation. Regardless, these providers do offer some advantages, particularly to smaller suppliers that may not be able to afford big technology expenditures on their own. Here are some key supplier benefits to registering on a third party supplier network, as promoted by Ariba:

- Suppliers can more efficiently do business with existing customers by reducing transaction costs and facilitating the exchange of content and transactions over the Internet.
- You only have to register once to do business with any corporation that uses a particular online supplier network.
- You can receive orders in your preferred order formats, including Commerce XML, EDI, HTML, fax, or e-mail.
- You can continue to use your current e-commerce infrastructure and still participate in a third party network.
- Smaller suppliers without sophisticated e-commerce capabilities can use this infrastructure to do business with large corporations—publishing online catalogs and receiving orders over the Internet.
- Everything is tracked, simplifying reporting and record-keeping. Third party platforms route orders securely and reliably. Suppliers receive order notifications as well as transaction histories and full audit trails. All stages of the transaction process are protected and reported.[viii]

Technology Tip #8: EDI, EFT and ERP are your friends.

Another commonly requested requirement for suppliers doing business with large corporations is Electronic Data Interchange (EDI) software. EDI gives suppliers the ability to exchange virtually all information—from job specifications to purchase orders to invoices, to shipment notices to credit memos to financial projections—with the corporation.

The advantage of EDI is that it eliminates vast amounts of paperwork (and time), thus lowering costs for both the supplier and the corporation. If you learn that EDI is required by one of your corporate prospects, perform a cost analysis to determine if you should purchase the EDI software yourself or outsource this function. Another advantage of EDI is that it involves a standard process, so you can learn a lot simply by reading an EDI manual—which may even be provided by your corporate customer.

One component of many EDI systems is Electronic Funds Transfer (EFT). Even if EFT is not required, Pamela Chambers O'Rourke wisely recommends that GMEs implement it with their corporate customers. This way, your payment goes directly into your bank account and you never have to endure the stress of being told "the check is in the mail." These days many of us pay our home bills (such as phone, electricity and cable) online, so you should request the same of your customers. EFT is the fastest way to get paid—now that is incentive to embrace this technology!

ERP (Enterprise Resource Planning) is a protocol suppliers may have to support to do business with a large corporation. Examples of ERP systems include SAP, Oracle, PeopleSoft and J.D. Edwards. ERP is an integrated software solution used to manage a company's resources and business management functions, such as business planning, inventory/materials management, engineering, order processing, manufacturing, purchasing, accounting and finance, human resources, and more. Companies use ERP systems to integrate all departments within a company while simultaneously linking the corporation to its customer and vendors. The objective of an ERP system is to help a corporation monitor and control its overall operations. As with any technology, research your corporate customers to learn if you will need to integrate with their ERP system in order to do business with them.

Technology Tip #9: Going once…going twice…many companies are going to online reverse auctions.

Reverse auctions are real-time bidding competitions among pre-qualified suppliers to win a customer's business. These auctions occur on the Internet using specialized software. Bidders submit progressively lower priced bids during the scheduled auction time. Unlike a traditional auction in which bids go higher, the winner of a reverse auction is often the company that submits the lowest bid.

While this sourcing tool has been around for less than 10 years, it has already gained widespread acceptance.[ix] The clear downside to reverse auctions is the feeling that you are competing solely on price. Reverse auctions are certainly not for all suppliers, so be sure to study them carefully before participating. Many firms pre-qualify bidders so that they know the low price bidder also has the capacity to deliver as well as a reputation for quality and service.

If you do decide to participate in an online reverse auction, Billie Bryant of CESCO, Inc. advises you to figure out your profit margin and "just how low you can go" before ever logging on. Then, just be aggressive, she says. Reverse auctions are not hard; just be careful not to get excited and allow your price to drop too low.

Technology Tip #10: Outsourcing may be necessary.

WBE Avis Yates Rivers, president and CEO of Technology Concepts Group, Inc., says that her biggest challenge in servicing corporate customers is hiring and maintaining the technical talent that is necessary to supply companies with differing technological requirements. The question is tricky: How do you know if it is a good investment to hire technical employees when you do not yet know if you will have enough corporate business to support the resources required?

In response to this challenge, Avis suggests that GMEs partner with a firm (or firms) that can supplement your own resources, therefore creating greater bandwidth. Or, you may need to consider partnering with one or more firms that can complement your company's technological resources with different ones that they possess. Look to your certification organization or professional association for potential partners. According to Avis, you may want to consider outsourcing the following services on a temporary or permanent basis:

- Payroll and benefits administration
- Network engineering
- Premises wiring (data cabling for local area networks)
- Disaster recovery/backup, in case your system crashes
- Another challenge is augmenting your internal systems with different protocols dictated by various corporate customers. As Avis and others have told me, there is a cost factor that typically does not get passed on to the customer, but is the cost of doing business with big companies. These costs begin to mount as you add new and different customers. What to do? Avis' solution is to outsource specific job duties to firms that specialize in those areas. This works well if a corporation requests a highly specific software application or customization that does not require a full-time staff person, but rather a one-time-only expert. Look for a temporary staffing firm that specializes in technology personnel. There are several WBENC- and NMSDC-certified companies that fit the bill.

If you do opt for outsourcing, WBE Colleen Perrone, president of The Caler Group, Inc., points out the importance of finding someone you trust, and offers a great suggestion for finding the right vendor: "When first setting up our computer intranet and Internet configurations, I met a lot of computer technicians who would charge enormous sums for operations that did not work. On about the fifth try, we found a vendor who stated that if he could not do the job right, he would charge us zero! With nothing to lose, we hired him on a contingency basis. He was not only successful, but has also been with us for nine years. His honesty and integrity have helped us to maintain state-of-the art technology." Who could argue with that result?

Regardless of how much technology work you outsource, it is important to train your own employees in basic technology. Billie Bryant trains all of her staff in software applications in order to provide the best customer service possible. A technologically savvy staff performs more quickly, saving everyone time and money.

Final Words on Technology

The three most important takeaways from this technology primer are to:

- Be honest, but unapologetic, with any corporate buyer about your technological capabilities.
- Research your customer's requirements and needs.
- Actively show your willingness to adapt to a corporation's requirements.

The good news is, once you prove your ability to work within the technological requirements of one big company, it is much easier to adapt to—and win business from—others.

Now, finally, it is time to pull together all of the work you have done so far—online, offline and inside your head—to make your case to the corporate customer of your dreams. It is time to plan your pitch.

Chapter Seven

The Second "P" of Supplier Diversity Success: Planning and Presenting Your PITCH

You have secured the meeting with the decision makers at a major corporation. You have assessed your pricing and technology. It is time to seal the deal. This chapter focuses on key advice for pitching to a major corporation and coaching you through the preparation of a compelling, comprehensive, content-rich presentation. Then the following chapter will sharpen the communication skills you will employ on The Big Day.

Presentation Content

Now that you are prepared to discuss the important issues of pricing and technology with your corporate prospects, get ready to combine this with the rest of the information you have gathered to this point about your customer, your competitors, your current clients, and, of course, your own business. All of your hard work will result in nothing unless you can persuasively communicate it during your sales pitch.

As a successful business owner you have no doubt designed many new business pitches in your career, but, as you have learned already, presenting to corporate America has some unique challenges. Particularly when you are bidding against an existing supplier, you need to be sure your presentation addresses the key metrics by which you will be assessed. But, fear not. As you have learned thus far in this book, there are many people in the supplier diversity community willing to lend their help to make sure your presentation is as strong as possible. Below you will find some of the best advice in the business.

Remember above all else that the way you prepare, deliver and follow up your pitch indicates to a corporation how you will treat them as a customer in the future, so do your absolute best and never cut corners.

First, Get Personal

I highly recommend that all GMEs develop customized materials for every corporate pitch presentation. Always create targeted media kits and Power Point presentations, and you may even want to design a special brochure or other professional "leave-behind" targeted to the corporation you are pitching. Make it clear that you are not recycling a pitch made to another company.

Customization does not just mean including the target company's logo on your presentation materials. It means including the company's terminology, key words and common acronyms in your presentation or proposal. It means reading up on the company's recent activities in the news and on the Internet for several days leading up to your meeting. Show your potential new corporate partner that you have done your homework, and that you have done everything you can to learn about their company.

Personalizing your presentation includes:

- Featuring the company's correct name and logo in your presentation materials. Be careful—spellings (Deutsche Bank), hyphenations (Bristol-Myers Squibb Company) and post-merger combinations (DaimlerChysler, ExxonMobil) can be especially tricky and can change.

- Including key words or phrases from the corporation's mission statement or goals and objectives—and then tying this language to *your* company's mission and goals. Visit the company's supplier diversity website for ideas.
- Using industry buzz words to show that you are on the cutting edge of your field. Again, comb through the website of the corporation you are pitching to make sure your terminology matches theirs, particularly when it comes to technology.

Getting personal also means getting to know the corporation's existing products and services with your five senses. This advice comes from the book, *Perfecting Your Pitch*, by WBE Nancy Michaels, president of Impression Impact. According to Nancy, many smart businesspeople who pitch their products or services to a large company overlook the most obvious form of research—the "live, in-person, real-world" kind she likes to call "Research Unplugged." Here is some of her wise advice:

"If your prospect is a retail store, shop there. If your prospect is a cosmetics line, wear it. If your prospect is a production company, see their films. If your prospect is a regional bank, visit their ATMs and tellers. If your prospect makes pencils, use them whenever you write. At the very least, you should call and ask for the annual report of every company you are targeting (many annual reports are available online as well).

"Take notes every time you visit a location, call the company, or have any other interaction. Do not forget to enter your findings in your database. This is information that senior-level people will value when you are pitching your services for improving their current practices and increasing their competitive advantage. Make notes about your experiences and note how your product or service can improve the lives of your potential clients…and use this in your pitch."

A "Small" Mistake Can Cost You Big

Carol Martin, former director, Supplier Diversity for Sears, Roebuck and Co. cautions, "Many GMEs make the mistake of approaching our buying organization and my office with the introductory statement: 'My company is a certified small business…' It is important to understand that the only people in a corporation who understand the significance of 'small' [as defined by the Small Business Administration certification] are those dealing in government contracting. In my corporation, that includes possibly only one other person besides me. Since more companies are seeking fewer, more significant supplier relationships, any reference to 'small' is an immediate kiss of death—working with numerous 'small' suppliers is counter to the direction of most large corporations. If a supplier chooses to identify as a diverse supplier, stating women or minority ownership is sufficient."

Concerned about the way you are describing your GME status? Practice your company description with your supplier diversity contacts or a mentor in your certifying organization. As you can see, even a seemingly "small" word can have big consequences.

Then, Get Specific

While all pitches are not the same and all suppliers may not be asked to address every issue imaginable, you must be prepared for any and all questions. I have surveyed many corporations to learn the factors they assess when evaluating new business pitches.

Kathy Homeyer, corporate supplier diversity coordinator at UPS, recommends that all GMEs be prepared for "the $64,000 question":

"If I buy your product or service, how will it help my company to gain a competitive advantage?"

Can you answer that question for all of your potential customers? What specific, measurable value do you bring to the table for this corporation? As Joan Kerr from AT&T explains, "Nothing is more compelling than a supplier who says, 'I understand the challenges of your industry and I can help you be more successful.'" Consider how much less persuasive it is to say, "We make products for call centers" than to say, "My company offers a proprietary quality check software for call centers that has proven to improve satisfaction by 30 percent."

Show you have done your homework and are prepared to deliver what the company needs:

Cheat Sheet: What the Buyer Wants to Know

Include the following topics in your pitch to present the most comprehensive and impressive information possible:

Customer Focus – As mentioned throughout this book, show not only that you will treat your corporate client like gold, but also that you have done your research to fully understand the needs and goals of the company. Then, of course, demonstrate that you are a perfect match for their needs.

Specialization – Exhibit your core competency in the area you are pitching. Share your experience and expertise. Be specific.

Cost Savings and Value Add – With today's constant focus on cost-cutting and streamlining, be sure to show that you are as focused on efficiency and profitability as your corporate prospect. As WBE Heather Herndon Wright advises, you need to show that you can provide at least one or more of three simple, but critical, components to the supply chain: 1) Cost Reduction; 2) Cost Avoidance; or 3) Increased Revenues. Otherwise you will have a very hard sell.

Innovative Business Solutions – Are you on the cutting edge in your field? Corporations want to know that their partners are continually improving their products and services. Show that you have a track record of innovation and a commitment to maintain your competitive edge.

Technology – You must demonstrate that you are technologically savvy and able to interact with the technology used by your corporate partner. As mentioned in the technology section of this chapter, many companies require that you are using Electronic Data Interchange (EDI) or e-commerce for product purchases and payments. Do not wait for the company to ask about your capabilities. If you do not currently have the technological capability that you think (or know from your research) you will need, Billie Bryant advises that you show a proven track record of delivery in non-technological ways, e.g. with billing, invoicing or purchase order processing. Add to this your willingness to ramp up quickly, and you should impress.

Additionally, Gwendolyn F. Turner of Pfizer notes that impressive technological capabilities can help make a smaller supplier appear like a larger company. "It is good marketing to show that, as a 'little guy,' you can deal with our company in the same way as a 'big guy' can. You may have more opportunities if your technology makes you appear bigger than you are."

Quality Processes – Share some information about your business processes and operations management. If you are ISO 9000 certified, make certain that fact is front and center on all of your marketing materials.

Recognition – Demonstrate any examples of excellence in your business, such as awards and certifications, particularly from industry or GME organizations familiar to the corporation you are pitching.

References – Share your best references to show that you have a proven track record and clients eager to vouch for you. Do not be shy about demonstrating that you have other corporate buyers. Corporations are actually pleased to know that you are already working with big partners and that you are able to provide multiple services to multiple customers.

Strong Finances – You must prove that you are in good financial condition. Corporations do not want to think you will go broke without their business. Although you may not offer them for close scrutiny, do attend the meeting with financial statements or budgets that may be relevant to the contract you are discussing.

Compliance – Depending on your industry, do not neglect to show that you fulfill such requirements as Occupational Safety and Health Administration (OSHA) product and service safety standards.

Readiness – You need to be ready, willing and able to provide the products or services you are pitching. Could you deliver right away if necessary? Remember never, ever to promise something you cannot deliver.

Finally, Get Comfortable

Customized, thorough content is crucial, but even the best information can be ineffective if it is communicated poorly.

Great content can appear just okay if it is not presented with confidence.

Practice Makes Perfect

Even if you believe you have excellent presentation skills, you must practice (and practice and practice) before you present in front of corporate buyers. Reach out to your network and employees for guidance and feedback before the big day.

First, practice your message with your existing clients. If you have developed a good relationship with a satisfied client, he or she will likely be happy to listen to the key points you plan to make with a large corporate buyer and flattered that you sought their advice. Satisfied clients are a good judge of what you do well and what made them contract with your company. Do not be afraid to ask for their support.

Second, practice your entire pitch in front of a "mock corporation," made up of anyone you know who has worked in the higher levels of a Fortune 500 company. Consider your staff, friends and family or mastermind group members. You might also invite fellow WBEs who have made pitches to the same corporation or a similar-sized company to review your presentation. Most communications experts also recommend that you video tape (or at least audio tape) your practice sessions so you can critique yourself.

If you believe you need to get professional assistance to improve your presentation skills, you can take a public speaking class at your local community college, join a group such as Toastmasters or hire a communications coach (another opportunity to work with a fellow GME). Many professional associations, including WBENC, also offer classes and workshops on communication and presentation skills.

When you practice, ask your audience to evaluate your pitch on the following factors:

- Clarity of your message – Are you explaining your company and its value proposition or services clearly and concisely? Have you controlled the dialogue and presented what you believe is important about your product or service for this targeted corporation? Some industry jargon helps you prove your expertise, but beware of overlong, overly detailed explanations.
- Capabilities – Does the audience believe that you are capable of doing the specific business you propose to do with the large corporation?
- Presentation style – Are you projecting a confident, strong and positive persona? Do you have any quirks or ticks that may be distracting to your listeners? Do not let anything get in the way of the message you want to convey. Watch for the following:
  - Too many uses of "um," "like" or "you know"
  - High-pitched or wavering voice
  - Too much hand movement
  - Not enough eye contact
  - Shifting from foot to foot
  - Nervous giggling or coughing
  - Speaking too quickly or too slowly
- Presentation materials – Are your presentation materials— PowerPoint, charts, product samples, etc.—professional, clear and necessary? Do they match your other collateral materials and offer a consistent image of your company? See the "Cheat Sheet" in this section for more tips on creating professional presentations.
- Typos and grammatical mistakes – Never, ever, ever, ever, ever tolerate typos or mistakes in your presentation materials or in your speech. Tell your practice audience not to be shy about pointing out any mistakes they see, or even think they see. This issue is, of course, even more important for GMEs

pitching services such as translation, communications, human resource consulting, advertising, or any other area that involves representing the corporation through writing or speech.

- Length – Is your presentation too long, too short? Do you get to your main points quickly enough? Remember, no matter how long your meeting is scheduled for, you may have significantly more or less time than you think. Be aware of how long each segment of your presentation takes so you can adjust if necessary during your meeting.
- Tone – Are you presenting in a positive way? Are you focusing too much on negatives or challenges and not enough on positive solutions? A little humility is nice, but do not undermine your credibility by appearing pessimistic or overly self-deprecating.
- Certification – Have you highlighted the advantages you bring to the table as a certified business?

Cheat Sheet: Tips for a "Perfectly Presentable Presentation"

Marketing and pitching expert Nancy Michaels shares tips on presentation visuals from her new book, Perfecting Your Pitch (Career Press, 2005):

- Create professional presentation materials. The beauty of today's technology is that it creates a level playing field for small businesses and independent salespeople. Even the "small guys" can create presentations with impressive visuals and some (but not too much!) animation. Not proficient with technology yourself? Hire an expert or even a smart high school or college student to help with your graphics.
- Do not use more than two font types in your presentation.

This confuses the eye and draws attention away from your message.

- Use lighter letters on a dark background. This is more visually appealing than black letters on a plain white background.
- Avoid writing out exactly what you are planning to say—this is the biggest mistake presenters make. Never read the words exactly as they are printed on the screen. This is the surest way to put your audience to sleep. You know your stuff! Use visual images to enhance the words you are planning to say.
- Use numbers, statistics and diagrams. Impressive numbers are often more compelling than words when it comes to a business pitch. This is crucial if you know that key financial managers will be in the room during your meeting.
- Do not outline every project you have ever done for each of your 20 clients. Instead, use testimonials to build your case. A single glowing sentence from each client testifying to your value (again, use numbers that show cost savings and added value) will be sufficiently impressive. And remember to include your clients' company logos with their testimonials. This is especially important if you have completed work for well-known companies in your industry—brand names really stand out in a presentation. (Be sure to obtain approval from your current or former clients before using their names in your presentation.)
- Provide meeting attendees with a printed list of references, including all contact information. Be prepared with this information before your prospect asks for it. This shows confidence and planning on you part. Again, confirm with your references that this is okay.

I can attest that Nancy practices what she preaches. WBENC has contracted with her to present her "Making the Pitch" and

"Perfecting the Pitch" workshops to WBEs at our national conference as well as at matchmaker meetings around the country. I had seen Nancy present her "generic" workshop to the WBENC audience, so I was surprised and impressed when, at a presentation at a matchmaker held at the UPS headquarters in Atlanta, her presentation was subtly different. Interspersed throughout her talk were references to UPS that were current and relevant to the supplier diversity and purchasing nature of the event. It was clear she had done her homework. In addition to setting a good example for the audience, Nancy impressed the senior executives at UPS who were present.

Anticipating Questions

While you cannot anticipate every question you will receive during your meeting, there are some common questions asked by corporate buyers in virtually any industry. Practice your answers to the queries below. You may want to consider including some of this information in your prepared presentation:

- Tell us a bit about the history of your company. (This is a great opening to draw attention to your certification.)
- Who are your key clients?
- Why do you want to do business with XYZ Company?
- Have you worked with other large companies?
- What are your biggest weaknesses?
- How quickly can you ramp up to integrate with our systems?
- What systems does your company use for invoicing, order confirmation, etc.?
- What is your geographical service area?
- Do you drop ship?
- Are you willing to subcontract to one of our prime contractors?

- Do you have a supplier diversity program in your company?
- What percentage of your spend is with diverse suppliers?
- Do you give volume discounts?
- Can you provide custom packaging?

Pitch Meeting Dos and Don'ts

- **DON'T assume your certification will win you the business.** Never walk in with a sense of entitlement because you are a GME or a certified business. Your certification may have gotten you to this point, but your business acumen and value proposition will get you the rest of the way.
- **DON'T overpromise.** This point is worth repeating again. While this is a sales pitch and you should always put your best foot forward, there is no advantage to exaggerating your capabilities. If you promise an unrealistic time frame or deliverable, you will lose the business. If you continually find that you are unprepared for the requirements corporate buyers are seeking, you may need to reassess your readiness for supplying to this market and set your sights a bit lower until you can expand or improve your capabilities.
- **DO show your enthusiasm and passion.** You may be small compared to the corporation you are pitching, but large companies know that one of the advantages of working with entrepreneurs is the passion and drive they bring to the table. Let your enthusiasm shine through.
- **DON'T bring too many giveaways or gadgets.** Corporate buyers will not be impressed with flashy gifts or gizmos emblazoned with your logo. On the contrary, they may think you are frivolous in your spending on such items. In fact, if they are too expensive, or appear to be expensive, accepting them may violate the ethics policy or code of conduct of the company.
- **DO take notes.** Note taking shows that you are not just

interested in pitching your products or services, but that you want to be an active partner with the corporation. Notes will also remind you of key messages to include in your follow-up.

- **DON'T interrupt.** Some presenters are so eager to give every word of their prepared and much-practiced presentation that they power through, ignoring questions, visual cues or comments from their audience. Remember that the goal of your meeting is to win the business, not to win an Oscar.

- **DON'T cling to an outdated value proposition.** Pamela Prince-Eason of Pfizer reminds GMEs not to continue to pursue a particular type of business when the purchaser tells you it is no longer part of the corporation's strategy. All businesses experience change over time and often large growth leads to implementation of new strategies. For instance, many corporations have moved to managed service provider structures for services such as temporary IT labor in order to most effectively manage these resources. If a company determines a particular structure is best for its business, then a potential GME supplier should look for a way to work within the new strategy, instead of clinging to old value proposition. Do not pitch a product or service that no longer matches a company's business model.

- **DON'T offer to work for free.** This tip also comes from Pamela Prince-Eason and her colleague, Gwendolyn F. Turner. "We do not like it when someone offers to do work for free. We understand that the supplier is trying to prove himself or herself, but offering work for free makes the work appear less valuable."

- **DO stay open to detours.** The meeting may turn in an unexpected direction. Buyers may take a strong interest in a product or service that surprises you. When their questions and interests are in an area that you can fulfill, be open to opportunities you may not have expected. Just take a deep breath and *listen* for their interests.

- **DON'T be stingy with your materials.** Bring more than enough print-outs of your presentation (so meeting attendees can take notes and follow along) and your marketing materials. Do not let anyone feel neglected, even if they arrived late and unannounced.

Test Your Technology

Planning to use PowerPoint, an LCD projector, a laptop, a VCR or any other high-tech or low-tech product during your presentation? Do not leave anything to chance. Never rely on the company to provide you with *any* support, including an electrical outlet. The best plan is to arrive prepared to give your presentation in an empty room. Bring all presentation and technology needs along with you, and, as Nancy Michaels noted, know how to use them. Take a minute or two at the beginning of your meeting to politely test your technology. (Even better, the company may allow you to enter the room a few minutes early to set up.)

I am always shocked and dismayed when I attend a conference and the speaker clicks on her remote...and clicks...and clicks...and nothing happens. It is inexcusable to waste precious minutes of your time in front of a buyer fiddling with your laptop. Be 110 percent prepared, even if it means taking a lesson from your 15-year-old on the workings of your VCR. I cannot emphasize this point enough—it detracts from your credibility to seem like a person who cannot work your own presentation technology. If it is totally beyond you, or makes you nervous, bring a staff person with you to handle the technology. If handled seamlessly, this can add to your presence as the leader and eliminates unnecessary distractions. That will leave you free to concentrate on the message, not the medium. And, it goes without saying how horrifying this would be if you were pitching

HP, Microsoft, IBM, AT&T or another high tech corporation. If you are pitching those companies, make certain that your systems are theirs and not the competitor's!

One last note: bring extra batteries and light bulbs. "Murphy's Law" is alive and well. If all else fails, be prepared to be calm, cool and collected if you have to revert to a high touch, low-tech presentation without the planned technology. Since you cannot guarantee the size of the room or whether or not your laptop will crash five minutes before your presentation, hard copies are a must for backup. The new key chain drives are perfect for backing up a presentation or other material. They plug into the USB port of any computer and can fit in your pocket or purse.

Recently, a WBENC consultant, Julie White of McKinley Marketing, thought she was prepared for all events when presenting to a strategic planning session of our Board of Directors. She traveled from Washington, D.C. to San Ramon, California, for the meeting. Not only was the presentation on her computer, but it was also backed up to a CD in the event that the computer crashed. Julie had been careful to keep everything right with her in her carry-on luggage, not trusting the airline to lose the important presentation. After hopping off the shuttle bus at the rental car agency, she was horrified to discover that her bag was not on the bus—a look-alike was in its place and her bag had apparently been inadvertently, but critically, taken by a traveler who, it was discovered, was en route to Brazil! The bag was recovered and the presentation saved, but Julie aged ten years in the process.

If you are calm about any technology snafus, the buyer will be impressed with your confidence rather than sympathetic about a botched pitch. You can use the situation as an occasion to show your professionalism and grace under pressure. Never lose your cool.

Image Matters

In the rush to put together a presentation, fly to a different city, call your kids at bedtime and return fifty e-mails on your BlackBerry, it is easy to "let slide" some elements of professionalism and poise; but now is the time to be on your best behavior. Remember that decision makers are considering a long-term relationship with you. They are paying attention to *everything* you say and do as well as the image you project.

Talk the Talk...Politely

When you are involved in a formal sales presentation, always err on the side of formality, manners and professionalism in your language. Even if you feel you have a good rapport with the people in the room and you are excited about offering them the Best Product Ever, avoid using even mild profanity or slang. While the content of your presentation—cost, value, etc.—is of the utmost importance to your listeners, the way you speak will also be observed.

Pamela Prince-Eason tells the unfortunate story of a GME who arrived for a pitch meeting in Pfizer's impressive office in midtown Manhattan dressed very casually. "This business owner offered a very good price, but her overall style was too laid back. While she may be able to do business in other parts of the country, she must come across in a more professional way in order to do business with our company. When pitching to Pfizer, wear a suit. Speak professionally. Stick to the facts. Avoid colloquialisms. Different audiences may require different styles, so know the culture you are entering and respect its protocols. If you are unsure of the culture in a company you are pitching, ask your supplier diversity contact.

Clothing and Accessories

I know I sound like the schoolteacher I once was, but you must pay attention to your grooming. It is simple, but we often forget how much physical appearance matters in a presentation. Wear your best and most conservative suit (and have it dry cleaned and pressed), polish your shoes, carry a professional briefcase or tote bag, and make sure your hair and nails are neat, clean and tailored. If you have a pin representing your certification or an industry association, wear it. Okay, end of lecture.

Be Extra Careful with Brand Names

- Do not use a Dell laptop to present to IBM.
- Do not carry a Nokia phone into a meeting with Motorola.
- Do not use a Staples notepad in a meeting with Office Depot.
- Never tell an executive at Canon that you will "Xerox" a document for them.
- And please do not FedEx a presentation to UPS.
- Note that I would not mention this issue if no one had ever made these mistakes. Do not let this happen to you!

Before You Leave

Do not be afraid to ask for the sale! Never leave a pitch meeting without knowing your next steps.

Do you need to meet with someone else in the company? If so, request the correct name and contact information and ask what the process is to get you in front of that person. Should you contact the person directly or will your supplier diversity advocate set up the meeting for you? Will he or she come with you to the meeting? If appropriate, ask for tips on what to emphasize in that next meeting. Find out how much time will be allotted to that next meeting.

Do you need to send additional information or product samples? Clarify what is required and where and to whom it should be sent.

Do you need to provide additional information about your company—financial statements or additional references, for example, before a decision will be made? Make certain you ask about and understand the due diligence process. If you have done your research, talked to other vendors, and posed the right questions, you will not be surprised and should not be offended by the questions asked or the materials required. Some GMEs have expressed offense when asked to provide financial information that they view as confidential. You should understand, however, that your financial stability is important to a company that is considering entering into a business relationship with you. Your product might be used as part of a larger process and if you cannot deliver because you do not have the cash flow to pay workers or order materials, then the company and other vendors in the supply chain will be at risk.

Lastly, ask when you will hear back and whether you will be called or if you should follow up. Do not forget to say thank you for the time and opportunity to meet with the contact. If you have followed the above tips and provided a compelling pitch, you may be on the verge of breaking through a tremendous door to opportunity!

After the Meeting

The pitch does not end when you leave the building. Remember to send a personal thank you note to every attendee as well as your supplier diversity contact. Most people believe that a hand written note is the most effective. Try to include appreciation for a particular comment or action that is associated with the meeting. For example, you might write:

Dear Robert:
Thank you for taking time from your busy schedule to meet with me and my team on Friday. Your advice on the

timing of our approach to the regional widget buyer is greatly appreciated and will help us to craft our next presentation. I look forward to hearing back from you the first of next month on next steps. In the meantime, call me personally with any questions or thoughts on things we may not have covered that will assist you in getting us that appointment.

Sincerely,

Jane Supplier

If you have promised to follow up with additional information, product samples, references or other materials, make certain that you follow through completely and in a timely manner. Also prepare for the likelihood that your initial sales pitch will be the first of several meetings with various decision makers in the corporation. The process of selling your products or services to a major corporation can take quite a long time and a large amount of follow up and patience. Hence, the next chapter and the third "P" of supplier diversity: perseverance.

Chapter Eight

The Third "P" of Supplier Diversity Success: PERSEVERANCE

An ounce of patience is worth a pound of brains.
– Dutch Proverb

A common question I hear from GME business owners is, "How long does the entire process take, from applying for certification to obtaining a corporate contract?" The answer, of course, is that the time frame varies widely depending on your business size, your industry, which corporations you are targeting, the overall state of the economy and good old fashioned luck. The only guarantee is that the process is bound to take longer— sometimes a year or more—than most go-go-go entrepreneurs would like. Remember the fishing metaphor from Chapter Three? Well, both fishing and corporate procurement require enormous patience, and the perseverance to keep casting your line.

It is my belief that most things in life that are worth having do not come easily, and corporate contracts are no exception. I promise you that GMEs with large corporate contracts will agree that any delay they experienced in the procurement process was more than worth the ultimate reward. Good business is always worth waiting for.

Here is a personal story from my days as the first woman manufacturers' representative in the textile industry. The largest prospect in my six-state New England territory was Bradlees

Department Stores, with literally hundreds of stores throughout New England and the mid-Atlantic states. I could not get an appointment to meet with the buyer to discuss my lines and why they were a fit with the Bradlees' customer. My salvation was that Bradlees had what seems now to be a very progressive policy, something called "open buying days." Any sales representative for any company could show up, sign in and wait to see the buyer. (Of course, you had to do some research ahead of time and know which buyer you wanted to see.) This could involve a wait of ten minutes or several hours, but, eventually, they had to meet with you.

I called on Bradlees during these open buying days once each month for 18 months before I got my first order with the company. I tried to have something new to pitch each time and was always eager to listen to the buyer's explanation of what was currently selling in his stores. Of course, I paid regular visits to the stores as I traveled the territory to get a feel for the changing product mix, seasonal variations and price points. The next time around, I incorporated that knowledge into my pitch. Over time, the buyer grew to believe that I understood his customer and was looking for the second order, not just the first. As the first woman in the industry and the only woman sales rep calling on him, I also showed that I was more than a novelty, I was around for the long haul and my business was apparently stable if not thriving.

The commission on that first sale was more money than I had earned the entire previous year. That one company had more stores than all my other clients in the territory combined. The way I looked at it, the opportunity to market to hundreds of stores in one visit was well worth the persistence. Success is frequently defined by not quitting before the "yes."

The Waiting Game

Let us first understand why the corporate supplier diversity process can potentially take several months to several years. Here are some factors that will affect your contract:

- **Timing** – As discussed several times throughout this book, corporations only purchase certain products at specific times of the year. They may not even buy every product every year. However, they may request proposals many months before they actually plan to purchase a particular product or service. If this is the case, your supplier diversity contact or the purchasers themselves should inform you of their time frame.

- **Corporate Processes** – The bureaucratic nature of large corporations means that many people are likely involved in the decision to work with you. The simple fact that one vice president is away on vacation can set your contract back by several weeks.

- **Budgets** – It is no secret that corporations have been in serious cost-cutting mode for the past several years. Large expenditures can be subject to the ups and downs of the company's balance sheet.

- **Strategic Sourcing** – The corporation may already have a supplier for your product or service. Part of the purchasing decision may be as to whether you provide sufficient differentiation to move the contract to you, or whether they may want to refer you to the prime as a Second Tier subcontractor. The upside is that you may be pleasantly surprised to find that they want you to do more than you initially propose.

- **Due Diligence** – Many companies conduct significant due diligence on your company before entering into a relationship. As discussed earlier in this book, your ability to fulfill on a contract is critical not only to your own success, but to that of your corporate customer as well.

How will you know what your time frame may be for an answer from the company you have pitched? LISTEN. Listen for comments about the process, next steps, challenges and time lines. Procurement professionals know that you are eager for a contract so they usually (but not always) do their best to manage your expectations. While there is not much you can do to speed up the decision-making process of a potential corporate customer, you can and should do everything you can to stay on the company's radar screen. Sometimes the wait may be considerable. The WBENC-sponsored *Access to Markets Study*, conducted by the Center for Women's Business Research and released in early 2003, found that the average corporate contract is re-competed only every three years. It seems an eternity, but if you are in business for the long run, you will want that contract in two or three years as much as you want it now.

If you do experience a long wait, think of ways to stay on the buyer's radar screen. This is where what you have learned in earlier chapters comes into play. Network in the areas where the buyer networks. Be certain to say hello. Send press releases and announcements of new contracts, especially those that are relevant to the particular industry. Schedule periodic meetings to discuss possible new opportunities in the company or expansion of the current contract that might provide a subcontracting opportunity. In short, do all the things you might do if the order were just around the corner. Your competitor might go out of business or just out of favor, new opportunities might arise, or a referral to another company might be in order.

It is also crucial that you not do anything that might actually *hurt* your chances at this stage of the game. Remember that the way you conduct yourself during every step of the procurement process shows the corporation how you do business. Do not bad mouth the supplier diversity executive or purchasing official, no matter what you think of them. Do not go over their heads and complain that you are not getting business. Do not discuss your experience with other contacts in competing companies. In other words, do not become emotional. Remember that this is business, not personal.

While You Wait...

- Check your references before your client does. Have a third party check you out so that you neither put someone on the spot that does not feel comfortable recommending you, nor get a reference that is less than you think you deserve.
  - Call first and ask if you can use this person as a reference.
  - Prepare a list of points that you believe are important to stress and ask if you might e-mail it to make the referrer's job easier.
- Keep a tracking file of what you have sent, when you sent it and whether a note, e-mail or product sample generated a response.
- Be sure to track your e-mail and phone communications as well whether or not you received a response.
- Identify other corporations in the same industry to see if you can maximize your marketing strategy and research and market to them as well. You can never count on a corporate contract's coming to fruition, so do not put all of your eggs in one basket. Surely you have been pursuing several potential customers all along, so one deal will not make or break your year.

Once you have provided a potential corporate client with everything they have requested—a proposal, an in-person pitch meeting, references, product samples, etc.—your mantra should become "perseverance and patience." To revisit my earlier speed dating metaphor, remember that the goal is not a hot date but a long-term relationship!

Perseverance means:

- Keep your supplier diversity contact in the loop at all times, even if he or she was not present at the pitch meeting. If you have any questions, you might contact this person first, rather than nagging the person making the decision to purchase your products or services. In most cases, your supplier diversity contact can inform you of the time line for the company's decision so you have an idea of when you can expect an answer.

- Perseverance includes a large dose of hard work. In other words, now is not the time to pray! SHE helps those who help themselves. If you are concerned about your ability to carry out a corporate contract, spend this time working on a plan for how you can deliver on your promises. Work closely with your advisers, staff and others who will be helping you manage this large client when the deal goes through.

- You should absolutely share good news and also be honest about any changes that may affect the corporation if they choose to do business with you. Honesty and forthrightness are crucial when you are building trust with this new partner.

- Keep all of your certifications and memberships up-to-date. Do not lose a potential contract because you have forgotten to renew your certification.

Patience means:

- DO NOT BE A PEST! Calling or e-mailing your corporate contacts every day will not help your cause at all. Jackie LaJoie of Merck identifies "too much contact too often" as a mistake often made by impatient GMEs. It is better to find a balance and work on developing a relationship for future opportunities.

- Maintain your relationships with other suppliers to the

company and other industry leaders. Do not drop all of the contacts you made while networking because you are waiting for a decision on a corporate contract.

- Continue to network and show up at industry events. I got the first contract with Bradlees, referenced earlier, immediately after running into the buyer at an industry trade show. The buyer saw me talking with a senior executive from one of the companies I represented and he was impressed by my level of access. It is never just one thing that leads to the sale, but rather an entire package.

- Keep excelling in the core competencies that attracted the corporation to you in the first place. This will only help when the contract finally begins. Send those updated press releases announcing your awards and new contracts.

- Rely on your mentor, association colleagues, mastermind group or other trustworthy people to help you through the waiting period. If you do not know any other suppliers to the particular company you are waiting on, contact your local certification organization to ask for an introduction to someone who has lived through the same process. It helps to speak with someone who has walked (and waited) in your shoes.

If Your Bid is Unsuccessful

Although we all hate to admit it, sometimes patience and perseverance are not enough. All pitches simply will not be winners. What should you do if your bid is unsuccessful? The best approach, of course, is to learn from the experience to maximize your chances of securing a contract in the future, either with the company that turned you down or with another firm. Here are some tips for regrouping after a setback:

- Request feedback – Yet again, the first place to go at this point is to your supplier diversity contact inside the company. This person is already invested in your success and is likely to be more honest and helpful when it comes to discussing a rejection. Do not whine, complain or criticize. Ask for constructive feedback that is as specific as possible so you can learn the reason why you did not win the business. Bids can be unsuccessful for a wide variety of reasons (e.g. price, timing, a more qualified supplier, withdrawn funding, personnel changes, etc.) so be sure to learn as much as you can so you can plan your next steps.

- Analyze your timing – Lisa Shevy, executive director of the Women's Business Enterprise Council – West, reminds GMEs that "no" may really mean "not now." Maintain contact with your supplier diversity contacts and department buyers to find out when new opportunities may be available.

- Sometimes—but only sometimes—you just have to give up. You may go quite far down a particular path that does not lead anywhere. If you find yourself frustrated and your calls are not being returned, it may be time to reassess your strategy and make sure you are approaching the right companies (and the right people and departments in those companies) with the right value proposition. Hopefully your supplier diversity contacts will alert you to truly impossible situations, but you will need to make the final business decision.

The good news is that, if you have carefully built strong relationships inside a company, you can keep each other abreast of changes in either of your situations that may open up a future opportunity to do business together.

When Your Bid Is Successful

If you offer a high-quality product or service, you have established and nurtured meaningful relationships and you have followed a targeted and persistent strategy for selling to a large corporate customer, success will eventually be yours. The phone will ring and you will hear that magical word, *"yes."* Congratulations! Securing a corporate contract has the potential to carry your business to remarkable heights and open extraordinary doors of opportunity.

One of the most enjoyable aspects of my job as president of WBENC has been the privilege to share in the celebration of successful owners of Growth Market Enterprises who, thanks to hard work and good business practices, see their greatest dreams come true. Read on for final thoughts on keeping the contract you have worked so hard to secure.

Success Story: Julie Levi, Founder and president, Progressive Promotions, Inc.

WBE Julie Levi is a master of persistence. Here she shares her inspiring story of business success in her own words:

When I first became certified five or six years ago, I got very excited and thought that every corporation in the world was going to want to do business with me and Progressive Promotions because I was woman-owned. So I got a list of all the companies in America that wanted to do business with WBEs. I thought, "This is going to be amazing. I am going to call everyone on that list because I am certified!" Needless to say, it was a huge waste of time and it took a while for me to figure out that this was not realistic at all.

I called Susan Bari and said, "I am just not having any success." She asked, "What are you doing?" I told her I was calling corporations to say they should do business with me because I am woman-owned. Susan said, "Julie, you need to pick five to fifteen companies that meet your business strategies, that you know you can serve really, really well, and focus on those."

So I started a very strategic marketing plan and did research on companies that would be my best potential customers: I focused on travel, hospitality, finance, creative services and consumer packaged goods. I picked companies that were geographically desirable and that fit our business strategy. And then I started to market to them only. I learned what was important to them and what promotional products they were currently using. I also researched how their business was doing. If they were laying off 1,500 people, then they would not be buying promotional products!

I also started to go to the WBENC conferences and began meeting supplier diversity people and procurement people who could get me the introductions to people at their companies who were in marketing or who procured promotional items. I was very focused and strategic. Sure enough, three years ago I met Lynn Boccio and Frank Gramo of Avis Rent A Car at a WBENC conference. I told them the Progressive Promotions story. They basically said, "You are nice, but there are a million promotional products out there and we already have a provider."

That did not dissuade me at all. Why not? They fit my profile! They were headquartered in New Jersey [where my company is based], they are in the travel and hospitality industry, they are receptive to WBE companies, they wanted to increase their diversity spend and they buy a lot of promotional products. And so I kept following up—with phone calls, sending my e-newsletter and showing them promotions I did for other clients related to the travel industry, such as American Express and Travelodge. I shared statistics from the industry. I sent them articles of interest. We got to know each other better, and I got to know their marketing people in the same way.

Six months went by, twelve months went by, and I kept doing the same. Eventually I got a call from an Avis marketing director. She said, "Julie, we are looking to change promotional product companies and we would like you to come in and present your story for our team." It was a year to a year and-a-half of very strategic marketing before I got that phone call. You have to earn the right to present your company!

I prepared extremely carefully for that appointment with Avis. You have only one shot. When I went in I presented a very strategic solution: I asked why they were looking to change companies, why they were unsatisfied. I asked, "What is the pain in your current situation?" They said that their current way of buying promotional products was very de-centralized, therefore they were not saving cost and their logo integrity was in jeopardy."

We analyzed their challenges and came up with an Avis Webstore, which provided 90 products that the salespeople could purchase online, including selected items to help them build their brand and increase referrals and sales. We included a special budget allocation feature for each buyer on the site to track purchases. Every month we provide a free reporting service so they can see exactly how much was being spent. We offered a strategic solution. At the end of the day, Avis liked what they heard. In our first year, 2005 to 2006, we were able to streamline their process, create really efficient reporting, reduce their costs tremendously and maintain and police their brand integrity. It was a beautiful solution.

To me, that is the beginning of the story of Progressive Promotions and Avis. We got our foot in the door. It was a nice program to start, but our goal is to penetrate our clients very deeply. With Avis we have now moved on to their human resources department and we are looking at international marketing. And on and on and on. Avis started as a contract of a few thousand dollars and in 2006 it will be over $1 million. We now have an entire team working on this account—a team that figures out their challenges and works on that all day long.

As you can see from Julie's story, persistence can really pay off!

Chapter Nine

Keeping the Contract

It is true that securing your first corporate contract can be one of the most exciting moments in your career—as well as one of the most daunting. Your first order of business is to take a deep breath and...celebrate! It is so important to take time out to pat yourself on the back when you reach a huge goal like winning a new corporate customer. Pop a bottle of champagne, schedule a long massage, throw a party for your employees or do something else that marks the occasion. You will not have much time for leisure once the contract fulfillment begins!

Get Started on the Right Foot

Here is a checklist of actions to take upon receiving a contract offer from a large corporation:

After you call your mother or significant other, call your lawyer, accountant and other important business advisors. A large corporate contract can change your business enormously, so call on experts to help you make a smooth transition with your new client. See the cheat sheet below for specific advice on negotiating your contract.

Cheat Sheet: Contract Law 101

In the excitement of a big offer, it is easy to agree to terms that you may regret later. Here are some key tips from Becky Troutman, an attorney with Thelen Reid & Priest, LLP, so you can be educated about the legal issues your lawyer will be reviewing in your contract:

1. Understand your business requirements and get your legal team involved sooner rather than later, particularly where the contract relates to a request for proposal or an information technology purchase.

2. The contract should clearly state a vendor's performance requirements, including expected product capabilities, service levels and time frames.

3. Plan for change. If appropriate and to the extent possible, the contract should permit the customer to add or change volumes, use rights, licensing models, products and services on pre-agreed pricing terms.

4. Contracts relating to the development and use of any intellectual property, such as software and websites, require special attention. In general, work product created by an independent contractor is owned by the independent contractor unless the agreement states otherwise.

5. Include well-thought-out termination provisions. Under what circumstances should each party be able to terminate the relationship? Is it necessary or desirable to include a transition period requiring continued performance after termination for a certain period of time? What other rights and obligations should survive termination?

6. Read the boiler plate carefully. In particular, contract provisions relating to confidentiality, representations and warranties of the parties, indemnities, limitations on liability and dispute resolution may be one-sided and unacceptable.

7. Make sure you have meaningful remedies if the other party fails to perform.

• Show your gratitude. Do not pass "Go," do not collect $200 (or $200 million, for that matter) without pausing to thank every person who helped you win the contract. I advise writing personal thank you notes to any and all of the people who helped you win the contract: supplier diversity contacts, other internal corporate advocates, helpful professionals from your certification organization or association, strategic partners, references, employees and, of course, your mother. I cannot overemphasize the importance of saying thank you.

- Share your good news. Success breeds success, so make sure prospects know that you are winning business with other companies. After making certain that your new client has no objection to your sharing the good news, send a press release announcing your new business relationship to the media, existing and potential customers, associations and your certification organization. Regional certification organizations are a particularly great place to garner free publicity. WBENC and several WBOPs, for instance, publish "Done Deal™ " reports in their newsletters and on their websites, and the WBENC website features success stories right on its home page. Remember that supplier diversity executives regularly read such newsletters and websites—this free, targeted publicity is priceless. Do not forget to add the press release to your company's website as well.

- Add your impressive new customer to any client lists you feature on your website or in your media kit.

- Educate your staff on your new customer and the specifics of the contract. Company buy-in will go a long way toward providing excellent customer service across at all levels.

FAQ: What if my corporate customer is part of a merger or acquisition?

Mergers, acquisitions, takeovers and bankruptcies are a relatively common occurrence in today's business landscape. What does a supplier do when the corporation he or she is doing business with is involved in a merger? Definitely do not panic. Remember that a merger can represent entirely new possibilities for you and your business. If you learn of a merger, your first step, as always, is to communicate with your supplier diversity contacts. Find out as much as you can about the planned merger and how suppliers will be affected.

As AT&T began acquiring other companies, then supplier diversity manager Jackie LaJoie, and the supplier diversity team spearheaded the creation of a comprehensive supplier diversity transition manual that offered an A-to-Z guide on AT&T's supplier diversity policies, procedures and programs. The guide helped ensure smooth integration of supplier diversity into the new business entities.   A member of the AT&T supplier diversity team also used the manual to conduct personal orientation with new suppliers "inherited" from acquired companies. Likewise, as AT&T spun off some of its divisions into independent companies, those companies maintained the supplier diversity programs and policies that AT& T helped to either establish or strengthen.

That was 2004, and just two years later AT&T has merged with SBC Communications and it is SBC that, under the leadership of executive director of supplier diversity Joan Kerr, is taking the lead in integrating the diversity piece of the combined supply chain.

The entire telecom industry seems to be realigning (again) and has seen the recent mergers of Sprint/Nextel and MCI with Verizon as well as the AT&T/SBC merger.

If your corporate customer experiences any large shift, your first course of action should always be to communicate with your supplier diversity contact or other trusted person in the company. Do not panic—communicate. Depending on your product or service, the changes can bring you in contact with new corporate opportunities, even new industries in which to market. Jackie LaJoie, mentioned above, is now with the pharmaceutical firm Merck. Her former colleague, Fernando Hernandez, is at Washington Mutual, as is former Lucent employee Johnny Lewis.

In another example, WBE Leslie Saunders, of Leslie

Saunders Insurance & Marketing, became concerned when Cendant (the parent company of Avis Rent A Car) acquired Budget Rent A Car. "I had a training contract with Avis when Cendant acquired Budget, and there was a consolidation of vendors and contracts. There was a time when I thought I would be eliminated from the process."

Leslie immediately made contact with her supplier diversity advocates: Lynn Boccio, Frank Gramo and Robert Bouta, SVP of Properties and Facilities. "They went to bat for me," says Leslie. "Even Bob Salerno, the CEO, went to bat for me. I worked out my contract and now I have a relationship with both Budget and Avis, and there is room for more growth."

In addition to awarding business to Leslie, Cendant has helped grow her business by sponsoring her attendance at the Tuck-WBENC Executive Program presented with the Tuck School of Business at Dartmouth and supporting her nomination to the Advisory Board of the magazine Enterprising Women. During a merger or acquisition, a little communication goes a very long way.

Best Practices for Keeping Contracts

As you will learn, GMEs are often quite willing to share advice with fellow corporate suppliers. Here are some tips on keeping the contracts you have worked so hard to win:

- Stay connected to all of your networks for support. Nikki Olyai of Innovision Technologies, Inc. advises GMEs to continually seek counsel. She recommends that GMEs always stay true to themselves and seek insight and support from each other and from experienced business leaders.

- Ask your new corporate customer about a formal mentor/protégé program. According to a 2001 WBENC study, about one-quarter of the Fortune 1000 provides mentoring for WBE suppliers.

- Pay close attention to your responsiveness at the beginning of a contract. Return all phone calls and e-mail messages promptly so your new customer feels very comfortable doing business with you. This is particularly important for businesses located in a different time zone from your corporate customer. Emphasize the importance of timely responses to your staff as well.

- Be willing to give up short term successes sometimes in the interest of long term relationships. This advice comes from Amy Birnbaum of Royal Coachman, who provides chauffeured transportation services to major corporations, including Cendant. "We parallel our goals to our corporate clients' goals," says Amy. "We've dealt with the gas crisis and the [New York City] transit strike, snow, ice, etc. That leads us to communicate with our corporate contacts and individual contacts. If, for instance, we need to reduce costs in the short-term to win more of their business, in the long-term that's a positive for us."

- Track and communicate measurable results. WBE Carmen Castillo, president of technology company Superior Design International, Inc. (SDI), shares this story of how demonstrating results to a customer can increase your own bottom line: "When asked to develop and implement automation for a Fortune 50 customer, SDI embraced the challenge. SDI's task was to bring cost savings and enhanced usability through efficiency-generating web-enabled processes. The customer's input proved invaluable in conceptualization stages, and we worked closely throughout the design and implementation of an enterprise-level web portal.

  "SDI's automation produced dramatic reductions in program-based transactional errors. Prior to the web system, the program relied on manual processes that generated a historical error rate of approximately four percent. Within 90 days of SDI's web portal deployment, this error rate was reduced to less than one percent. With our technology, SDI has successfully sustained this dramatic reduction in error percentage across a high volume, North American initiative, allowing for the expansion of performance guarantees and growth of our business profitability with the customer."

- Continue to market your products and services to additional divisions in the corporation. Gwendolyn Turner praises the ongoing marketing efforts of one particular WBE who has done business with Pfizer for over 15 years. This particular WBE understands that Pfizer operates in a decentralized environment, so she markets herself to specific departments as well as cross-functional business groups within the large corporation. According to Gwen, this WBE's secret to success is that she consistently demonstrates the value and cost savings she has provided to Pfizer. She has made many contacts in the company and maintained them for years. "Now," Gwen reports, "other people within the corporation ask about partnering with her."

  Likewise, be sure to continue marketing products and services that your new customer may not yet be purchasing. As appropriate, regularly remind purchasers and supplier diversity executives of your additional capabilities. Debbie Faraone of The Elements, Inc. even found that the supplier diversity department of one of her corporate customers needed her services itself!

- Keep showing up. As so many stories throughout this book have demonstrated, the business owners who network, participate in events and maintain their relationships are the ones who consistently win business. Corporations are proud to do business with visible, successful figures in the supplier diversity community, particularly those whom they see at WBENC and NMSDC events. The more you show up, the more you are top-of-mind when new business opportunities arise.

The End...and the Beginning

I hope that this book has inspired you join the thousands of American entrepreneurs who have grown their businesses to extraordinary levels by becoming certified and doing business with corporate America. As you have seen, the road is not always smooth, but the rewards are abundant. Beyond financial success, most women and minority business owners say that the most rewarding aspect of being part of the supplier diversity community is the people they have met—from diversity professionals to association executives to fellow women and minority business owners across the country. I completely agree. I am proud to spend my days working with the inspiring men and women in the supplier diversity industry and the visionary leaders of Growth Market Enterprises around the world—people like you.

Thank you for all that you do for your employees, your customers, your communities and your country. I salute you.

Afterword

Women are transforming the face of business—and nowhere is that more evident than in business ownership. For all the entrepreneurial women reading this book, you are part of one of the defining trends of the past 15 years—the growth and expansion of businesses owned and operated by women.

As of 2004, almost 30 percent of all privately held firms in the United States are woman-owned (with 51 percent or more ownership by a woman or women). Your firms are making a major contribution to this nation's economic health and competitiveness through both job creation and revenue generation. As of 2004, these woman-owned firms are providing jobs for 9.8 million people and are generating close to $1.2 trillion in revenues.

Women are seizing the opportunities offered by entrepreneurship. Between 1997 and 2004, woman-owned firms grew at nearly two and a half times the rate of all U.S. privately held firms (23 percent vs. 9 percent).

However, the story of women's entrepreneurship is about more than the number of business start-ups. It is about the expansion in revenues and employment, which far exceeds the growth in number. While the number of majority woman-owned firms increased by 23 percent between 1987 and 2004, employment increased by 39 percent and revenues skyrocketed 46 percent. Clearly, woman-owned businesses are larger, more substantial and making a greater contribution to the economy with each passing year.

Entrepreneurship is an equal opportunity phenomenon. Women of all ethnicities are starting businesses and, as of 2004, there were 1.4 million businesses owned by a woman of color, growing at six times the rate of all businesses.

Women are starting businesses in all industries, with the fastest growth in what might be considered "non-traditional" industries for women—construction, agribusiness, transportation/communications/public utilities, and finance/insurance/real estate. This trend in industry diversification is especially pronounced among the larger businesses owned by women, those with $1 million or more in revenues. The larger businesses owned by women are more likely to have large corporations as customers, suggesting that marketing to corporations provides an impetus for growth.

Women are making great strides in overcoming the hurdles confronting them as business owners. While access to capital, access to technical expertise and networks and access to markets remain key challenges, perhaps the most pervasive challenge is that of being taken seriously. That is why it is so important to have the hard data about the strength of women's entrepreneurship. These numbers tell the corporations, financial institutions, policy makers, media, and, most of all, ourselves that woman-owned businesses are, indeed, to be taken very, very seriously as an economic force.

Over the past decade, women business owners have benefited from many passionate champions. Foremost among these leaders is Susan Bari. For more than a decade, Susan has been instrumental in ensuring that women are viewed as full players in this nation's economy with commensurate access to opportunities. This book, the culmination of years of experience, will be the textbook for all who want to grow their enterprises by doing business with corporate America.

To all the readers of this book, my best wishes for much success.

Sharon G. Hadary, Ph.D.
Executive Director
Center for Women's Business Research

For more information on woman-owned businesses, visit our website, *www.womensbusinessresearch.org.*

Resource Guide

Here are some useful websites for more information on various topics covered in *Breaking Through*. Please note that WBENC assumes no responsibility for, nor does it endorse, the information contained in any of the websites mentioned.

Associations, Networking Groups and Organizations

American Society of Association Executives
www.asaenet.org

American Subcontractors Association (ASA)
www.ASAonline.com

Center for Women's Business Research
www.womensbusinessresearch.org

Institute for Supply Management
www.ism.ws

International Franchise Association
www.franchise.org

Latino American Management Association (LAMA)
www.lamausa.com

Latin Business Association (LBA)
www.lbausa.com

National Association of Minority Contractors
www.namcline.org

National Association of Small Disadvantaged Businesses
(NASDB)
www.nasdb.org

National Association of Women Business Owners (NAWBO)
www.nawbo.org

National Association of Women in Construction
www.nawic.org

National Black Chamber of Commerce
www.nationalbcc.org

National Center for American Indian Enterprise Development
(NCAIED)
www.ncaied.org

National Indian Business Association
www.nibanetwork.org

National Minority Supplier Development Council (NMSDC)
www.nmsdcus.org

National Society of Black Engineers
www.nsbe.org

National Women's Business Council (NWBC)
www.nwbc.gov

Native American Business Alliance
www.native-american-bus.org

U.S. Chamber of Commerce
www.uschamber.org

U.S. Hispanic Chamber of Commerce
www.ushcc.com

U.S. Pan Asian American Chamber of Commerce
www.uspaacc.com

The Veterans Corporation
www.veteranscorp.org

Women's Business Enterprise National Council (WBENC)
www.wbenc.org

Women Construction Owners & Executives, USA (WCOE)
www.wcoeusa.org

Women Impacting Public Policy (WIPP)
www.wipp.org

Women in Franchising
www.womeninfranchising.com

Women in Technology International (WITI)
www.witi.com

Women Presidents' Organization (WPO)
www.womenpresidentsorg.com

Government

Central Contractor Registration
www.ccr.gov

Minority Business Development Agency (MBDA)
www.mbda.gov

The Federal Marketplace
www.fedmarket.com

U.S. Small Business Administration
www.sba.gov

U.S. Department of Commerce (USDOC)
Office of Small Disadvantaged Business Utilization (OSDBU)
www.doc.gov/osdbu/

U.S. Department of Transportation (USDOT)
Office of Small Disadvantaged Business Utilization (OSDBU)
http://osdbuweb.dot.gov

Women-21.gov (a partnership of the U.S. Department of
Labor and the U.S. Small Business Administration)
www.Women-21.gov

GME and Small Business Publications & Websites

American Indian Report
www.americanindianreport.com

Asian Enterprise
www.asianenterprise.com

Black Enterprise
www.blackenterprise.com

Diversity Inc.
www.diversityinc.com

Diversity Information Resources
www.diversityinforesources.com

DiversityBusiness
www.diversitybusiness.com

Enterprising Women
www.enterprisingwomen.com

eVenturing
www.eventuring.com

Hispanic Business
www.hispanicbusiness.com

Latina Style
www.latinastyle.com

MBE (Minority Business Entrepreneur)
www.mbemag.com

Minority Business News USA
www.minoritybusinessnews.com

Small Business Television
www.sbtv.com

WE: Women's Enterprise USA
www.weusa.biz

Appendix A

WBENC Balanced Score Card

2005 Search for America's Top Corporation for Women's Business Enterprises
Part II: Balanced Score Card for WBE Program Process Improvement

Instructions

Section A – WBE Supplier Participation: Complete the blue box first. Use 6% as the "desired state" for WBE participation and prorate 25 points accordingly. For example, if your corporation achieved 6% or more WBE participation, your score is 25 in Section A; if your corporation achieved 5% WBE participation, your score is 21 (5% divided by 6% = .83; .83*25 points = 21 points). Note, the goal is to minimize the amount of spend excluded from the base. In general, it is common to omit the following types of spend: employee reimbursements, taxes, royalties. Additional exclusions (like insurance, employee benefits, utilities, rent, etc.). should be minimized and carefully evaluated on a case-by-case basis *to ensure there is absolutely no opportunity* for considering woman-owned suppliers for that particular category. Remember, once a category is defined as an "excludable," you have, in effect, closed the door to potential consideration for any woman-owned business in the future.

Section B – Manages WBE Supplier Relationships: This section refers to the extent to which the company proactively manages its relationships with woman-owned businesses. For example, corporations generally measure the performance of their largest suppliers. *The objective here is for at least some of your WBEs to be included in this process to document their added value as suppliers.* Complete the blue box first, add the total points for your company, and insert into "Company Score" for Section B. For example, if your corporation formally tracks the supplier performance of ANY woman-owned businesses in your supply chain, ten points are awarded. If your corporation tracks cost savings for ANY woman-owned businesses, another five points are awarded. If your company proactively facilitates the growth of ANY WBE suppliers, another 10 points awarded, for a total of 25 points in Section B.

Section C – WBE Program Sustainability: This section is detailed on pages two through four of the score card and refers to how the process is structured and positioned within your organization, including strategies employed to drive performance. Complete pages two to four by scoring points for the various activities your company has engaged in. Add the total number of points from pages two through four and insert in Section C on page one of the Score Card.

Section D - Links to Revenue: This section refers to the extent your corporation has leveraged integrating WBEs into the supply chain to generate sales/revenue. Documenting supplier diversity's impact on market share: 1) increases internal buy-in, 2) promotes innovative approaches to integrating and building the capacity of woman-owned businesses, 3) drives additional resources to continue integrating WBEs into the supply chain, and 4) builds brand equity with targeted customers to sustain and/or increase market share.

If your company sells to the government and/or other corporations that require women's business development, and your company FORMALLY tracks this revenue, insert "15" into your company score. Or, if your company provides products/services sold to individual consumers, and your company FORMALLY tracks the amount of sales/revenue generated from women as consumers, insert "15" into your company score.

2005 Search for America's Top Corporation for Women's Business E   nterprises
Part II: Balanced Score Card for WBE Program Process Improvement

Strategic Initiatives

Strategic Objective		Measure	Maximum Score	Company Score
Strengthen the Supply Chain	A	WBE Supplier Participation	25	
	B	Manages WBE Supplier Relationships	25	
	C	WBE Program Sustainability (see following page)	35	
Grow Revenue	D	Tracks revenue from WBE/Women Consumer Market(s) AND/OR corporate/government accounts	15	

Detail for A (WBE Supplier Participation):

2004 Total WBE Spend Tier 1		$
2004 Total WBE Spend Tier 2		$
# of 2004 Active WBE Suppliers		
Top WBE Supplier Spend as % of Total Base Spend		%

		Maximum Score	Company Score
% WBE Spend to Total Spend	%	25	

Detail for B (Manages WBE Supplier Relationships):

	Maximum Score	Company Score
Tracks WBE Supplier Performance Metrics	10	
Tracks WBE Cost Savings	5	
Facilitates Growth of Targeted WBE Suppliers	10	

Detail for D (Grow Revenue):
Check which applies:
Consumer Market _____
Government Market _____

Total 100 [ ]

SB Services

September 2005   Developed by SB Services, Inc. for WBENC.   Page 2

2005 Search for America's Top Corporation for Women's Business E   nterprises
Part II: Balanced Score Card for WBE Program Process Improvement

Strategic Objective	Measure	Maximum Score	Company Score	
Strengthen the Supply Chain	WBE Program Sustainability			**CEO Commitment**
		1		Corporate Policy Statement promoting the use of WBEs
		1		Active CEO leadership and involvement within the corporation
		1		Corporate WBE Goal
		1		Goals by Department or Commodity
		1		Cross Functional Leadership Team or Advisory Council
				Accountability for WBE Goals At All Levels
				WBE Program Performance linked to performance reviews and/or com pensation for:
		1		Some Buyers
		1		All Buyers (if all buyers are included, score 2 points 1 above and 1 here)
		1		Senior Purchasing Management
		1		Cross Functional Management (i.e., internal customers outside of procurement)
		1		CEO/President
				Program Structure
		1		Full time employee to drive the initiative
		1		Requires 3rd party certification with mandatory site visit that designates a t least 51% *female* ownership and control
		1		Requires 3rd party certification that includes a site visit (i.e., WBENC)
		13		Sub-Total This Page

SB Services

Developed by SB Services, Inc. for WBENC.   Page 3

2005 Search for America's Top Corporation for Women's Business E   nterprises

Part II: Balanced Score Card for WBE Program Process Improvement

Strategic Objective	Measure			
Strengthen the Supply Chain	WBE Program Sustainability	Maximum Score	Company Score	
				Proactively Managing the Supply Chain cont'd.
		1		Spending with WBEs increased over the last 12 months (or last f iscal year)
		1		Volume with the largest WBE exceeds .5% of Total Base Spend
		1		Maintains internal directory of active WBE suppliers
		1		Second Tier Process with required participation
		1		Incentive for meeting objective and/or penalty for non -performance
				WBE Outreach
		1		Facilitates WBE registration on corporate internet website
		1		Conducts in -house vendor fairs to introduce WBEs to buyers
		1		Participates in national/regional WBE trade fairs
		1		Sources WBEs through industry trade groups/organizations
		1		Maintains internal directory of potential WBE Suppliers
		10		Sub-Total This Page

35		**Total Score for WBE Program Sustainability**

SB Services
bridging boundaries

239

Appendix B

WBENC Women's Business Organization Partners (WBOPs)

WBENC has 14 Partner Organizations across the country that handle certification for all 50 states, as well as provide support and resources to WBEs on a local level.

Women's Business Development Center/ Florida
11205 S. Dixie Highway, Suite 101
Pinecrest, FL 33156
Phone: (305) 971-9473
Fax: (305) 971-7061
Web: *www.womensbusiness.info*

Georgia Women's Business Council
231 Peachtree Street, NE
Suite 300
Atlanta, GA 30303
Phone: (678) 904-8470
Fax: (678) 904-8474
Web: *www.gwbc.biz*

Women's Business Council Gulf Coast
1701 6th Avenue N., Ste. 469
Birmingham, AL 35203
Phone: (205) 321-4791
Web: *www.wbcGulfCoast.org*

Women's Business Development Center/Illinois
8 South Michigan, 4th Floor
Chicago, IL 60603
Phone: (312) 853-3477. Ext. 12
Fax: (312) 853-0145
Web: *www.wbdc.org*

Women Presidents' Educational Organization - New York
155 E. 55th Street, Suite 4H
New York, NY 10022
Phone: (212) 688-4114
Fax: (212) 688-4766
Web: *www.wpeo.us*

Women Presidents' Educational Organization – DC
1120 Connecticut Avenue, NW
Suite 1000
Washington, DC 20036
Phone: (202) 872-5515 x.18
Fax: (202) 872-5505
Web: *www.wpeo.us*

Center for Women & Enterprise
24 School Street, 7th Floor
Boston, MA 02108
Phone: (617) 536-0700 x.222
Fax: (617) 536-7373
Web: *www.cweonline.org*

Women's Business Council - Southwest
2201 N. Collins, Suite 158
Arlington, TX 76011
Phone: (817) 299-0566
Fax: (817) 299-0949
Web: *www.wbcsouthwest.org*

Astra Women's Business Alliance
5 Centerpointe Drive, Suite 400
Lake Oswego, OR 97035
Phone: (971) 204-0220

Fax: (971) 204-0221
Web: *www.astrawba.org*

Women's Business Enterprise Alliance
1900 North Loop West, Suite 270
Houston, TX 77018-8100
Phone: (713) 681-9232
Fax: (713) 681-9242
Web: *www.wbea-texas.org*

Michigan Women's Business Council
2002 Hogback Road, Suite 12
Ann Arbor, MI 48105
Phone: (734) 677-1400
Fax: (734) 677-1465
Web: *www.miceed.org*

Women's Business Enterprise Council-West
1201 S. Alma School Road, Suite 5200
Mesa, AZ 85210
Phone: (480) 969-WBEC
Fax: (480) 969-2717
Web: *www.wbec-west.org*

Women's Business Enterprise Council-Southeast
35 E. Gay Street, Suite 501
Columbus, Ohio 43215
Phone: (614) 228-4150
Fax: (614)621-9222
Web: *www.wbec-se.org*

Women's Business Development Center/Pennsylvania
1315 Walnut Street, Suite 1116
Philadelphia, PA 19107-4711
Phone: (215) 790-5059
Fax: (215) 790-9231
Web: *www.womensbdc.org*

Appendix C

Mandatory Supporting Documents for WBE Application

I. General Information
o   Printed copy of your WBENC application
o   History of Business
o   Professional and business license(s)
o   Résumés of owners, board of directors and key management team
o   Copy of bank signature authorization card or corporate resolution
o   Current union agreement(s), if applicable
o   Sworn affidavit, signed and notarized

II. Owner Eligibility
o   Evidence of gender for woman (women) owner(s) (copy of passport, birth certificate, or driver license)
o   Evidence of U.S. citizenship (examples include a U.S. passport, U.S. birth certificate or naturalization papers), *or* Legal Resident Alien status (a legal resident alien card)

III. Financial Structuring
o   Financial statements, including:
    - Profit and loss statement
    - Balance sheet for last complete year of operation or length of time business has been in operation (for a new business that has been in operation for less than one year, include the opening balance sheet)
o   Please submit copies of the following documents that are both currently active as well as any initiated within the three

years prior to this application:
- Debt instruments
- Equipment rental and purchase agreements
- Real estate leases

o   Three years income tax returns (includes *current and prior two years* federal income tax returns for the business. For businesses *less than three years old*, substitute personal federal income tax returns for the appropriate number of years.)

IV. Management Information

o   Please submit copies of the following documents that are both currently active as well as any initiated within the three years prior to this application:
- Management/consulting agreements (agreements that influence the management and/or operations of the applicant company)
- Service agreements (agreements that influence the day-to-day operations, including the production and/or distribution of the applicant's product or service)

o   Affiliate/subsidiary agreements (if the affiliate/subsidiary company is a WBE, please include a copy of the WBE certificate; *otherwise*, just include the agreement)

V. Personnel

o   List of all full-/part-time employees by name, position and length of service

o   Itemized employee payroll for the month prior to submitting this application (Note: this refers only to internal employees, not those who might be leased to/from other companies)

o   W-2s and/or 1099 forms for every officer, director or owner receiving compensation from the company for the most recent year

VI. Legal Structure

For Sole Proprietor

o   Assumed Name Documents

For Partnership
o   Partnership Agreements
o   Limited Partnership Certificate; if applicant is a limited part-
    nership, submit a certificate of existence and copy of the
    certificate of limited partnership issued by the state of forma-
    tion
o   Buy-Out Rights Agreement
o   Profit Sharing Agreements
o   Proof of capital investment by all partners

For Corporation
o   Certificate of incorporation
o   Articles of incorporation
o   Minutes from shareholders' first organization meeting and
    from first board of directors' meeting
o   Minutes from the shareholders'/board of directors' meeting
    establishing current ownership
o   Minutes from the most recent meeting of shareholders
o   Minutes from most recent meeting of board of directors
o   Corporation's bylaws
o   Certificate from the board secretary certifying the names of
    all current members of the board of directors
o   Both sides of ALL stock certificates
o   Stock transfer ledger
o   Proof of stock purchase or equity investment for woman
    (women) owner(s)
o   Voting agreements and other equity interests including stock
    options, warrants, buy/sell agreements and right of first
    refusal
o   If an out-of-state corporation, proof of authority to do busi-
    ness in the state where application is made
o   Schedule of advances made to corporation by shareholders
    for the preceding three years

For Limited Liability Company (LLC)
o   Articles of organization
o   Certificate of organization (for businesses in states that issue certificates)
o   LLC Regulations and/or Operating Agreement and/or Member Agreement
o   Member List with Titles
o   Proof of Equity Investment for Woman (Women) Owner(s)
o   If an out of state LLC, Proof of Authority to do business in the State where application is made
o   Schedule of Advances made to LLC by members for the preceding three years

Appendix D

Example of a Corporate "What We Purchase" Website

The following information appears on the UPS Supplier Diversity website at *www.community.ups.com/community/diversity/supplier/purchase.html.*

What We Purchase

 To keep our business running smoothly, we must purchase a variety of services and products. The services and products we purchase have been grouped into four categories: Services, Supplies, Equipment and Facilities. A detailed list appears below.

A Corporate Supplier Diversity Manager is responsible for ensuring our minority- and woman-owned suppliers have an opportunity to compete on an equal basis with all of UPS's suppliers. In our Corporate Office, the majority of purchases are made from our Materials Management Group. In our region and district offices, we have designated coordinators for our Supplier Diversity Program.

Services	Supplies
› Advertising	› Art/Graphics Supplies
› Art and Audio-Visual	› Audio tapes/Videotapes
› Artwork/Illustration	› Boxes
› Design	› Car Wash Supplies
› Packaging Design	› CD-ROMs

- Photocopy
- Photo Processing
- Presentations

Building Maintenance

- Carpentry
- Carpet Installation
- Electrical
- Fencing
- Heating and Air Conditioning
- Landscape
- Painting
- Paving
- Plumbing
- Roofing

Building/Janitorial Services Consulting

- Environmental/Civil
- Information Services
- Human Resources
- Marketing

Copier/Duplicating

Financial

- Banks
- Benefits
- Money Managers

Food/Vending Services

- Chemicals
- Data Processing Supplies
- First-aid Supplies
- Fuel
- Incentives/Premiums
  - Promotional Items
- Office Supplies
  - Copy Paper
  - Printed Forms/Labels
- Plastics
- Uniforms

Equipment

- Computer Equipment
  - Mainframe Computers
  - PC Computers
  - Telecommunications (phone systems)
- Office
  - Fax Machines
  - Furniture
  - Carpet
  - Lighting
  - Workstations
- Parts
  - Airplane
  - Automotive

- Graphic Design
- Leasing and Rental
- Legal
- Printing
  - Film Separation
  - Fulfillment
  - Mail Sorting
  - Offset
  - Silk Screen
  - Typesetting
- Relocation/Moves
- Security/Guard
- Temporary
- Training
- Video Production
  - Film/Videotape Duplications
  - Studio Services (Actors, Models, Voice Talent)

- Bearings
- Conveyor and Belt Systems
- Electrical
- Locks
- Nuts and Bolts
- Seals
- Tires
- Vehicle Purchases
  - Airplane Purchases
  - Forklifts
  - Ground Support Air Vehicles
  - Trailers/Tractors
  - UPS Package Cars (Trucks)

Facilities

- Architects
- Building Design
  - Construction or Renovation
- Facilities Management
- Leasing and Purchasing

Appendix E

WBEs Mentioned in *Breaking Through*, 2nd Edition

Introduction

Annette Taddeo
LanguageSpeak, Inc.
www.languagespeak.com

Chapter One

Barbara Singer
Barbara Singer Photography
www.barbarasinger.com
Barbara Singer is a New York-based photographer who has been producing sincere and natural portraits since 1983. Her background in fine art and her feeling for each person enable her to bring a fresh viewpoint and special techniques to the commercial world. "I look for the best in you to show with beauty and power," is her motto. Syndicated journalist Maximillien de Lafayette has written: "Perhaps, just perhaps, she is New York's best portrait artist-photographer....This superb photographer is a national gem." Certified by WBENC and the City of New York, she specializes in portraits for the corporate and advertising markets.

Linda Laino
Festive Productions, Inc.
www.festiveprod.com
Festive Productions is a special events production company that specializes in staging, lighting, sound, audio visual, mobile stage marketing, conventions, festivals, parades, galas and more. Festive Productions owns and operates all of its own equipment, which allows the company to pass savings on to its clients. Clients include, but are not limited to, Cendant, WBENC, WPO, The National Puerto Rican Day Parade, Inc., and The Hampton Classic Horse Show. This is a family-owned and operated company (a husband and wife team) that loves what it does and represents the spirit of special events. Festive Productions has been in business since November, 1997.

Anastasia Kostoff-Mann
The Corniche Group
www.corniche.com

Bonnie O'Malley & Cindy Sedlmeyer
ExhibitEase LLC
www.exhibitease.net
ExhibitEase provides visual presentation products, including exhibits, graphics, banner stands and custom and portable/modular displays for trade shows, events, recruiting, point-of-purchase and retail environments. The company also offers graphic design services, including 3-D, for all types of visual presentations and website design.

Nina Eisenman
Eisenman Associates Graphic Design and Advertising
www.eisenman.com
Eisenman Associates is a certified WBE that has been providing Fortune 500 corporations, as well as privately held

companies, with creative design and marketing solutions for over 40 years. The company specializes in the design of logos, websites, marketing materials, annual reports, brochures, advertising and presentation folders and graphics.

Betty Lau
Applied Information Services, Inc.
www.appliedinfo.com

Diana Conley
Advotek Inc. DBA/ComputerLand Downers Grove
www.advotek.biz
Advotek Inc., established in 1978, sells and supports computer automation for businesses and schools in the Metro Chicago area. The majority of the company's small and mid-sized customers dedicate their staff to their core business functions and delegate support of their information systems to ComputerLand Downers Grove. The company also provides quality and value through multiple services and multiple vendors. Services include: network integration, including wireless network installations; Internet data backup; system maintenance; project management; help desk; equipment leasing and equipment disposal.

Lynn J. Griffith, CMP
Welcome Florida, Inc.
www.welcomeflorida.com
Welcome Florida is an experienced destination management company and has been assisting corporations for the past 22 years by enhancing their meetings, conventions and incentives with customized services and creativity. Welcome Florida provides custom-themed events with creative décor and lighting, music and interactive entertainment, effective teambuilding and sophisticated challenges, all with in-house design and produc-

tion. The core of the company's business includes transportation, tours and activities, dining events, hospitality staff and event planning. Welcome Florida has been certified as a WBE for four years.

Sherra Aguirre
Aztec Facility Services, Inc.
www.aztec1.com

Rita Myers & Stacy Ames
Falmer Thermal Spray
www.falmer.com

Betsy Mordecai
MorEvents
www.morevents.com
MorEvents is a full-service global event management company specializing in events, hospitality services, meeting planning and specialty world-class sporting events. For more than five years, MorEvents has been a leading event management solutions provider to federal clients of all sizes, with two years of direct experience and success managing the President's Quality Awards. MorEvents has earned its success through a simplistic but creative approach to event and program management, the recruitment of exceptional individuals and adherence to the highest professional and ethical standards.

Amy Birnbaum
Royal Coachman Worldwide
www.royalcoachman.com
With service in cities around the globe, Royal Coachman Worldwide can accommodate any client's chauffeured ground transportation needs. Royal Coachman's customers value the company's one-stop shopping, high quality service and state-

of-the-art, time-saving technology.

Niki Beavers
JEVA Technologies
www.jevatech.com

Terri L.C. Hornsby
TLC Adcentives LLC
www.tlcadcentives.com
TLC Adcentives is a full-service promotional advertising firm. The company provides brand-building incentives that can be utilized as safety or employee incentives. It also supplies promotional products for special events, golf tournaments, company anniversaries and tradeshows and develops and implements full service company stores programs.

Chapter Two

Debbie Faraone
The Elements Inc.
www.the-elementsinc.com
The Elements provides quality, brand-recognized, creative product solutions. Clients look to The Elements for fresh, innovative ideas to reinforce and promote their company message and brand. In addition to being an ad specialty distributor, The Elements represents a variety of unique artists and distinguished retail lines, as well as designs and manufactures its own custom line of leather goods and writing instruments. Creative custom capabilities and marketing insight set The Elements apart. The Elements serves as a client's creative partner and adds value by focusing on every facet of a project, including quality control, packaging and fulfillment.

Leslie Saunders
Leslie Saunders Insurance and Marketing International
www.lsimi.com

Nancy Connolly
Lasertone
www.lasertone.com

Chapter Three

Pamela Moore
Ice Tubes, Inc.
www.icetubes.com

Rebecca Boenigk
Neutral Posture, Inc.
www.iGoErgo.com
Neutral Posture is the only certified woman-owned chair manufacturing company in the United States. The company manufactures ergonomic and multipurpose chairs and accessories. Neutral Posture is introducing a new line of industrial chairs in 2006, which will significantly expand the company's product line and distribution channels.

Julie Levi
Progressive Promotions, Inc.
www.progressivepromotions.com
Progressive Promotions, Inc. (PPI) is an 18-year-old, woman-owned, full-service promotional products agency dedicated to providing corporate clients with promotional ideas that yield strong and measurable results. Award-winning for creativity and service excellence, PPI develops ideas that will help its clients increase sales, build brand awareness, recognize employees, increase referrals, place media, create goodwill and

much more. PPI's service footprint is New Jersey, Illinois and California. Many of PPI's clients have offices nationwide that require regional offices to service these clients. PPI's prestigious client list includes American Express, Avis, Budget, Howard Johnson, Kraft Foods, Cartier and dozens of others. PPI's in-house services include hot stamping, engraving, pad printing, assembly, gift-wrapping and fulfillment, enabling them to offer quick service on last minute jobs. The company's creative and sourcing teams can develop concepts from idea to delivery.

Sharon Avent
Smead Manufacturing Company
www.smead.com

Smead Manufacturing is a worldwide leader in office filing products and records management systems. For 100 years, Smead has brought a spirit of innovation and integrity to keeping businesses and home offices organized. Smead's business principle is to provide quality products and solutions that best serve the organizational needs of its customers. Today, Smead manufactures thousands of organizational products designed to make paper and electronic document management more efficient and economical. From the introduction of color-coded indexing and efficient shelf-filing techniques to a comprehensive package of recordkeeping systems using integrated document management technologies, Smead continues to set the standard for state-of-the-art records management.

Nikki S. Olyai
Innovision Technologies, Inc.
www.innovisiontech.com

Innovision Technologies, Inc. is an advanced international engineering and information technology company of dedicated consulting specialists, applying a positive-minded, results-oriented approach to supporting its clients. Innovision

Technologies is dedicated to the highest level of quality, on-time delivery, competitive cost structure, technological foresight and continuous and proactive support. Innovision Technologies supports many Fortune 500 companies and is contributing to the continued success of several high-tech driven U.S. government agencies. The company was one of seventeen firms honored by the U.S. government, receiving the Outstanding Women Entrepreneur Award for being one of the best woman-owned businesses in the U.S. The company also received the U.S. Small Business Administration's Award for Excellence in 2002, and has been recognized by Congressional committees for outstanding leadership.

Leonor McCall-Rodriguez
Mira Promo, Inc. – Latino Speakers Bureau
www.latinospeakersbureau.com
Mira Promo, Inc. provides marketing, public relations and business support for successful Latinos who are on the international speaking circuit. Latino Speakers Bureau brings together authors, actors, scientists, business people and accomplished professionals from many walks of life to share a message of hope and success.

Melissa Mangold
Casco Manufacturing Solutions, Inc.
www.cascosolutions.com

Maryanne Cataldo
City Lights Electrical Co., Inc.
www.citylightselectrical.com

Barbara Bosha
Bosha Design, Inc.
www.boshadesign.com

Bosha Design provides inspired, effective design, delivering the strength and experience of a big firm, yet offering flexibility and individual attention. Bosha Design aspires to be a problem-solving partner working toward its clients' goals, and prides itself on delivering projects on time, and on budget. Whether the medium is the web or printed materials, Bosha Design, Inc. provides effective communications campaigns for businesses, educational institutions and other organizations. Competencies include corporate communications, branding, website, annual reports, brochures and direct mail. Clients can depend on Bosha Design's expertise to communicate ideas clearly and in a manner that will both entertain and effect response.

Christine Bierman
Colt Safety, Fire & Rescue
www.coltsafety.com

Colt Safety warehouses and distributes industrial safety supplies and personal protective equipment (PPE), providing head-to-toe protection for workers in hazardous environments, according to OSHA and NFPA regulations. The company's mission is to protect the American workforce by way of safety audits, product selection and placement, OSHA training and ongoing product service, maintenance and decontamination. Centrally located in the U.S., Colt ships coast-to-coast from a 30,000-square-foot warehouse. In 2005, Colt celebrated 25 years in business under the leadership of its CEO and founder, Christine Bierman.

Nancy Michaels
Impression Impact
www.impressionimpact.com

Terri McNally
Global Capital, Ltd.
www.globalcapitalltd.com
Global Capital, Ltd. provides equipment financing and leasing on all types of assets including technology, manufacturing and transportation. The company uses a consultative approach with its customers, listening to their tax, procurement and accounting guidelines and structuring transactions to meet their needs. Global Capital's payment schedules are structured to fit the cash flow needs of each client's business, offering fixed and floating rates and off-balance sheet financing. Global Capital offers the most competitive pricing in the marketplace and does business nationwide with small, medium and Fortune 500 companies.

Roz Alford and Nancy Williams
ASAP Staffing
www.asapstaffingllc.com
The company's mission is to provide quality service and expertise to its clients and consultants while delivering excellence to meet the needs of the industry. ASAP Staffing is a privately held, woman-owned corporation that has enjoyed strong, steady growth since December 1989. ASAP provides highly trained and experienced staff in specific technologies to Fortune 500 firms. ASAP also provides all levels of consulting including lan/wan/pc help desk support and administration, application development and maintenance, database design and project management. Regardless of the size or length of the project, ASAP utilizes an extensive database to provide client companies with the support they need. This network of consultants enables ASAP to respond quickly to its clients with the right technical resources the first time.

Heidi Berenson
Berenson Communications, Inc.
www.berensoncom.com

Berenson Communications powers up your performance whether you are facing the press, a presentation or a pitch. Berenson Communications harnesses its Emmy award-winning prowess to equip clients with tools and techniques that show instant results. From speeches to sound bites and from messages to mien, the company's unique media training and presentation coaching services fire up a client's natural talents while extinguishing the weakness.

Julia M. Rhodes
KleenSlate Concepts, LLC
www.kleenslate.com

KleenSlate Concepts brings new ideas to life. By working intimately with business, consumer and education customers, KleenSlate identifies new and emerging needs in the office supply and education market and customizes products to meet those needs. The company's priorities are idea innovation, customer satisfaction, honesty and dependability. KleenSlate's award-winning dry-erase product line facilitates and encourages fun learning and communication in schools, at home and in the office. KleenSlate Concepts expects to reach into several markets beyond education and office supply within the next two years. These include private labeling, promotional products, early childhood development, business, professional training, health-care, the restaurant industry, homes, and game and motion picture environments, as well as the fashion and entertainment markets.

Chapter Four

Marsha Rose Davidson
Telecopy, Inc.
www.telecopy.com

Telecopy is one of the leading CD, DVD and video duplication/replication companies in the Dallas/Fort Worth area. The company also provides custom packaging, fulfillment and drop shipment services. Since 1979, Telecopy's "old fashioned" customer service attitude and one-on-one relationships with clients have helped the company to evolve from VHS to CD/DVDs and remain on top in this ever-changing industry. Telecopy is active in its local WBENC council, The Women's Business Council Southwest, and partners with other WBEs in related services such as graphic design, video production and editing in order to supply a broad scope of services, thereby ensuring that Telecopy can provide solutions to its clients' duplicating challenges.

Mary Kay Hamm
Linden International
www.lindenint.com

Linden International, founded in 1981, is distinguished by its multi-year listing as a DIV2000 company, its president's appointment as a charter member of the Governor of Pennsylvania's Advisory Committee on Minority- and Woman-owned Businesses, and by its selection into the IBM Mentor Program, 2005-2006. From offices in Philadelphia, Dallas, Boston and Palm Beach, Linden teams with corporate and public sector clients to provide two services. The first is Linden's Procurement Services Provider offering, which delivers strategic sourcing projects that save real dollars while enhancing supplier diversity spend goals. Second, Linden's staffing service provides supplementary and permanent staffing to its clients' information technology, accounting, finance, and procurement departments.

Linden has unique competence in enterprise resource planning (SAP, PeopleSoft and Oracle), in staffing and running large accounting and finance projects, and in augmenting procurement during times of changing demand, such as mergers, acquisitions, and staff disruptions. Clients include major public utilities, global service companies, international pharmaceutical and personal care product corporations, and federal and state agencies.

Kerry Hammer
Hammer Press
www.hammerpress.com

Hammer Press is a full-service commercial printer. Starting with a comprehensive digital prepress department, the company's services include printing variable data and one-to-one marketing. Hammer Press can also print on materials such as plastic, Clingz, Magnacote and Unifoil. Packaging and a full-service mail house and fulfillment house, allow clients to keep their projects under one roof for full control.

Donna Cole
Cole Chemical & Distributing, Inc.
www.colechem.com

Michelle Boggs
McKinley Marketing Partners, Inc.
www.mckinleymarketingpartners.com

McKinley Marketing Partners provides seasoned marketing managers and communications resources to Fortune 1000 companies, government agencies, emerging businesses and trade associations. Woman-owned and operated, McKinley Marketing Partners provides services in most major metropolitan areas, including Atlanta, Chicago, Dallas, Denver, Los Angeles, New York, San Francisco and Washington, D.C. McKinley's marketing and communications managers join a client's staff when additional resources are needed to meet critical business initiatives when the work load exceeds available resources. McKinley maintains a roster of interim marketing managers (IMMs) who are ready to undertake projects for its clients whenever and for however long they are needed. Every IMM has tactical or strategic marketing expertise in one or more key industry segments. Across all industries, McKinley's IMMs have delivered solutions including advertising and public relations campaigns, lead generation programs, sales support initiatives, competitive assessments, channel and product launches, market research and more.

Sharon Evans
CFj Manufacturing
www.cfjmfg.com

CFj Manufacturing serves organizations across a variety of industries seeking innovative, cost-effective solutions for their employee recognition and promotional marketing needs. Established in 1983, CFj's products and services today include corporate service and safety awards, incentive and reward programs, branded merchandise, online stores and other business services ranging from uniforms and break room supplies to coffee, chocolate and bottled water. From its many global locations, CFj currently manufactures and distributes to over 160 countries worldwide. CFj has been honored with a variety of awards including the JCPenney National Supplier Diversity Development Award, the Frito-Lay "Other Goods & Services" Vendor of the Year, the Frito-Lay National Minority/Woman Supplier of the Year, the Boy Scouts of America National Award of Excellence, and the Women's Business Council – Southwest WBE of the Year award. In 2005, Sharon Evans was ranked #8 on *Fast Company's* list of the nation's 25 Top Women Business Builders.

Chapter Five

Lana Shannon
Chicks With Ideas
www.chickswithideas.com

Cynthia Wilson
Wilsonwest, Inc.
www.wilsonwest.com
Wilsonwest, Inc. is a woman-owned, industry-leading provider of event management and marketing-related services that focus on supporting Fortune 1000 companies' efforts to build lasting relationships with key business, employee and social contacts. The company's special events are designed to create an atmosphere and experience that foster high-touch client exchange, achieving each client's brand, culture and product/service demand objectives.

Sharon Cannarsa
Systrand Manufacturing Corporation
www.systrand.com
Systrand Manufacturing Corporation provides production and prototype machining of transmission, engine and chassis components using CNC equipment. The company is certified as TS 16949, ISO 14001 and Ford Q1, and is a Tier 1 supplier to the automotive industry. Systrand is a certified minority-owned and woman-owned company. The company has established a joint venture with ThyssenKrupp Presta for the grinding of camshafts. Systrand owns Systrand Korea, a machining company located in Busan, South Korea.

Karen G. McSteen
brandMatters, LLC
www.brandmatters.com
The brand strategy firm, brandMatters, helps clients

strengthen their business by strengthening their brand. The company offers a host of services, including workshops, market research, strategic planning and "brand cue" development. Clients range from The Ritz-Carlton Hotel Company to E! Entertainment. Karen McSteen, brandMatters president and former Marriott and AOL executive, is a leader in brand strategy; she is sought after to speak before associations and organizations about brand issues and brand trends.

Marilyn L. Bushey
Power Performance and Communication, Inc.
www.powerpacinc.com

Power Performance and Communication, Inc. (PowerPAC) provides executive coaching, facilitation and training to enable business owners to deliver on their vision. PowerPAC works intimately with small to mid-size businesses to develop detailed execution plans and deliverables to help translate vision into bottom-line results. Executive coaching sessions teach business owners how to translate their vision into definitive action plans with deliverables. Team facilitation helps focus the management team on collaborative goals accountability. PowerPAC is led by president Marilyn Bushey, who was honored as 2001 Advocate of the Year by the Women's Business Council Southwest and named 2004–2005 National Member of the Year by the National Association of Women Business Owners (NAWBO).

E. Denise Stovell
Stovell Marketing and Public Relations, Inc.
www.stovellmarketingpr.com

Stovell Marketing and Public Relations, Inc. is a full-service marketing and public relations firm, specializing in marketing strategy, public relations, content development and event management. The company has extensive experience developing programs for corporate America, women and minority business owners and nonprofit organizations.

Heather Herndon Wright
Herndon-Wright Enterprises

Katherine McConvey
KMM Telecommunications
www.kmmtel.com

Billie Bryant
CESCO, Inc.
www.cesco-inc.com
CESCO is a 38-year-old company located in Dallas, Texas. It is in the sales and service business of office equipment, supplies and furniture and is an authorized dealer and certified service provider for Xerox, HP, Lexmark and Brother. CESCO's partnership with major equipment manufacturers allows CESCO to perform as a prime contractor or a subcontractor. The company offers consulting services for choosing and right-sizing equipment and can also be utilized in facilities management contracts. The company offers training on digital connectivity devices in addition to soft skills and other technology training. In the office supplies business, the company's target market is primarily toner and other supplies that support all equipment. CESCO offers OEM compatibles in addition to remanufactured toner supplies. Other products include approximately 60 lines of furniture many of which are listed at *www.cesco-inc.com*. CESCO's revenue in 2005 was $6.5 million. The company's president is one of the founding members of the Women's Business Council Southwest and WBENC. CESCO is also certified by the North Central Texas Regional Certification Agency.

Mercedes C. LaPorta
Mercedes Electric Supply, Inc.
www.mercedeselectric.com

Mercedes Electric Supply (MES) is a woman/Hispanic-owned wholesale distributor of electrical supplies with 26 years' experience in the electrical supply business. The company is located in the heart of the South Florida market, with over 20,000 square feet of warehouse space and 8,000 feet of office space. MES is a distributor for numerous well-known electrical manufacturers, including Pass and Seymour, Osram/Sylvania, Square D Company & Lithonia. MES supplied electrical material for the Federal Law Enforcement Building in Dade County, Florida, the American Airlines Arena in Miami, improvements being done at Miami International Airport and the Broward County Civic Center, also in Florida. MES is an important supplier to many small and mid-size electrical contractors, as well as the large national contractors such as Turner/Austin and Fisk Electric. Currently, Office Depot and MGM Grand purchase electrical maintenance materials for their stores from Mercedes Electric Supply, Inc.

Chapter Six

Barbara Woyak
Future Trends Technology Management
www.fttm-llc.com

Future Trends Technology Management is a Scottsdale, Arizona-based provider of IT consulting and staffing, now serving clients nationwide. The company provides services including staff augmentation in all areas of IT, disaster recovery and business continuity planning, ERP and data center support.

Sandi Wietzel
Marketing Images, Inc.
www.marketingimages.com

Pamela Chambers O'Rourke
Icon Information Consultants, LP
www.iconconsultants.com

Icon Information Consultants, LP, headquartered in Houston, Texas, specializes in identifying and recruiting highly qualified information technology, accounting and finance professionals at all skill levels. The company's services include human capital solutions, consulting and payrolling, as well as a specialized project management division. Icon Information Consultants has gained its superior reputation by focusing its efforts on excellent customer service, timely and thorough responses and high values and ethics throughout the company. As a result, Icon has reached a "Top Tier" or preferred vendor status with most of its clients. Some of the company's top clients are Halliburton, HP, Lyondell/Equistar, Pitney Bowes, Schlumberger, Shell Oil Company, Enron, Nabors Drilling, Visa and Waste Management.

Avis Yates Rivers
Technology Concepts Group, Inc.
www.technologyconcepts.com

Founded in 1996, TCGI is a full-service technology provider delivering integration, infrastructure and project management services. The company's mission is to provide clients with information technology solutions that simplify complex needs in the workplace and improve efficiency, effectiveness, quality and compliance.

TCGI operates in every phase of the IT life cycle: strategy, plan, build, rollout and support. Few others match TCGI's capabilities, which include systems and network integration, convergence and infrastructure.

Colleen Perrone
The Caler Group, Inc.
www.calergroup.com
The Caler Group, Inc., a certified WBE, headquartered in Boca Raton, Florida, is a retained executive search firm. Founded in 1995 by Colleen Perrone, clients are nationwide and international. All of The Caler Group, Inc. recruiters are full-time employees with a business focus in the technology, financial services, consumer and energy industries.

Chapter Nine

Carmen Castillo
Superior Design International, Inc.

Endnotes

Chapter One

i.. "The Buying Power of Black America - 2003," *Target Market News, www.targetmarketnews.com*

ii. "Rise in Hispanics and Asian-Americans is Predicted," *The New York Times,* March 18, 2004.

iii. HispanicOnline.com

Chapter Two

iv. "The Leading Edge: Women Owned Million Dollar Firms," Center for Women's Business Research, 2004. www.*womensbusinessresearch*.org.

v. *www.nmsdcus.org/who_we_are/certification.html*

Chapter Five

vi. AECsoft USA, *www.aecsoftusa.com/sdg/main_faq.asp*

vii. Rutgers University, *http://procure.rutgers.edu/stsdp.html*

Chapter Six

viii. Excerpted from The Ariba Supplier Network, *www.ariba.com*

ix. Fein, Adam J., "Online Auctions are Here to Stay," *Modern Distribution Management* newsletter, 2004. (www.mdm.com)